Communication

The Key to
Effective Leadership

> *"Communication is the lubricant that makes organizations run."*
>
> — Lee Iacocca
> Former CEO of Chrysler Corporation

> *"The concepts of Process Communication complement Total Quality beautifully."*
>
> — Larry Adams
> Former president of Martin Marietta Corporation

> *"Being able to use the concepts of Process Communication is like having a magic wand."*
>
> — Marcene Franz
> Former vice president of U.S. Steel

Communication

The Key to
Effective Leadership

Judith Ann Pauley, PhD
and
Joseph F. Pauley

ASQ Quality Press
Milwaukee, Wisconsin

American Society for Quality, Quality Press, Milwaukee, WI 53203
© 2009 by ASQ
All rights reserved. Published 2009.
Printed in the United States of America.

15   14   13   12   11   10   09   5   4   3   2   1

Library of Congress Cataloging-in-Publication Data

Pauley, Judith A.
Communication : the key to effective leadership / Judith Ann Pauley and Joseph F. Pauley.
    p. cm.
Includes index.
ISBN 978-0-87389-767-9
1. Communication in management. 2. Leadership. I. Pauley, Joseph F. II. Title.

HD30.3.P39 2009
658.4'5—dc22

2009001749

Publisher: William A. Tony
Acquisitions Editor: Matt T. Meinholz
Project Editor: Paul O'Mara
Production Administrator: Randall Benson

ASQ Mission: The American Society for Quality advances individual, organizational, and community excellence worldwide through learning, quality improvement, and knowledge exchange.

Attention Bookstores, Wholesalers, Schools, and Corporations: ASQ Quality Press books, videotapes, audiotapes, and software are available at quantity discounts with bulk purchases for business, educational, or instructional use. For information, please contact ASQ Quality Press at 800-248-1946, or write to ASQ Quality Press, P.O. Box 3005, Milwaukee, WI 53201-3005.

To place orders or to request a free copy of the ASQ Quality Press Publications Catalog, including ASQ membership information, call 800-248-1946. Visit our Web site at www.asq.org or http://www.asq.org/quality-press.

∞ Printed on acid-free paper

Quality Press
600 N. Plankinton Avenue
Milwaukee, Wisconsin 53203
Call toll free 800-248-1946
Fax 414-272-1734
www.asq.org
http://www.asq.org/quality-press
http://standardsgroup.asq.org
E-mail: authors@asq.org

Dedication

To

Dr. Franklin Schargel, the past president of the Education division of the American Society for Quality, for his friendship, for sharing his leadership skills with us, and for recognizing how the concepts of Process Communication complement the concepts of Total Quality.

And to

Dr. Taibi Kahler, the clinical psychologist who made the discoveries on which the concepts of Process Communication are based, for his genius, for his friendship, and for improving our lives and the lives of all those we come in contact with every day.

Contents

List of Figures and Tables

Foreword

For those of you who do not know Joe and Judy Pauley, you are about to go on what the Beatles called a "Magical Mystery Tour." For those of you who, like me, have attended a Pauley workshop, you are about to renew a friendship.

If anyone can translate a visual session into a literary one, this book proves that Joe and Judy can. Few authors have the ability to build bridges between theory and application. The Pauleys do. They take the concepts of Dr. Taibi Kahler's Process Communication Model® and make it come alive with practical applications and easy-to-understand models. Basically, it is about leading by establishing positive relationships by:

- Helping people get their needs met positively

- Individualizing the way leaders communicate with everyone so that staff members and employees hear what they are saying

- Dealing with people in distress

- Helping leaders keep themselves out of distress so they'll be more effective

- Using the concepts of Process Communication to develop the leadership skills of their staff members and the strengths of their employees

- Using the concepts in private industry, non-profits, healthcare and education

As I read through the book, I said to myself, "This is the best chapter in the book" – until I read the next chapter. There aren't many books that I want to read a second time. This is a book you need to read twice. Maybe even a third time.

By the time you finish reading this book, you will have made two new friends – Joe and Judy Pauley.

Franklin P. Schargel
Education Division Chair, 2003-2005
American Society for Quality

It is truly an honor and exciting for me to introduce you to Process Communication and to Joe and Judy Pauley.

In 1993, when I expressed an interest in developing better leadership communication skills, a colleague recommended that I attend their Process Communication seminar. My colleague spent a few minutes explaining the concept of the "six-story condo" of personality. Then he went on to explain that it's possible to communicate in a way that each listener easily understands, and possible to assist when people are behaving in a dysfunctional manner. It simply made great sense!

I think that neither our families nor our schools provide us with the communication tools that are essential for developing strong and positive relationships. We do not understand the differences between or among people; instead of understanding, we develop negative and unhealthy attitudes and behaviors. Process Communication is a profound and useful tool for our communication tool bags.

I arranged to participate in a seminar the week before I was to assume responsibility for a dysfunctional department in a tertiary medical center. Every day following that seminar, I was grateful that I had attended and learned Process Communication. It was amazing to me how clear the concepts were and how easy to apply. It wasn't necessary to immediately master the process and make my communications perfect—and that was a shock! My staff and colleagues responded in such positive ways even as I began what seemed like baby steps toward improving my communication skills. Even more amazing? The members of our team recognized that I was making a difference and began to ask how I was doing it. They wanted to know my "secret." People from other departments across our health care system heard about our healthy behaviors and healthy environment and wanted to learn more. That desire to learn how to "Process" has been sparked in every location and position I have held since that time. People are hungry for ways to improve the quality of their lives at home and at work.

One example that still makes me smile occurred when I recognized a "rebel" on my staff. He wanted to wear an operating room cap that his wife had made for him, but the leadership of the operating room kept telling him no. As a result of this conflict, he became moody and a chronic workplace complainer. It is tough to motivate new staff when the experienced staff is already complaining about someone before they meet for the first time! I stopped the rebel in the hall one day to suggest that he put a disposable hat on over his own as he entered the operating room hallway and then remove it as he exited the hallway. I told him he was welcome to wear his own hat anywhere else in the hospital. He objected, saying that "they" wouldn't let him. I promised to support him and said that he should let me know if he experienced any harassment. Such a little thing! It turned him into a huge advocate for our department.

Another example was a "persister" in my department, an informal leader who consistently worked to oppose any action or recommendations by the formal leadership. I learned to ask him his opinions and listen to why he thought something was important. When I began to spend a few moments of my time listening and seeking clarification, he stopped being the source of problems in the department. It was a fascinating situation because it was not necessary to agree with him or to do things the way he would do them; it was only necessary to listen. This was another example of how a few minutes invested generated a huge return.

I could give you dozens of examples of how I have used Process Communication in a variety of circumstances. The most important thing I can tell you is that without Process Communication skills, I would not have enjoyed the leadership positions I was honored to have as the 22nd Chief of the Army Nurse Corps or the Acting Surgeon General and Commander of the Army Medical Department. The ability to develop a team, to support them and help them achieve their goals, is what makes leadership rewarding. Process Communication makes it easy.

Enjoy this extraordinary book written by fabulous, compassionate, loving people. Begin to implement the techniques even when you don't yet feel competent in their use and watch the positive response you will have from those around you.

Gale S. Pollock
Major General (Ret), CRNA, FACHE, FAAN
Executive Director Center of Ocular
Regeneration and Vision Restoration
University of Pittsburgh

Acknowledgements

We want to thank the leaders who provided the powerful stories contained in this book to explain how they have used the concepts of Process Communication in leading their organizations. Many of them are named. Several more are not, at their request. We are deeply grateful to all of them.

We also want to thank our colleagues around the United States who provided the introductions to many of the leaders quoted in this book. We especially want to thank Don and Pam Reed of Kahler Communications Atlanta, Brad Spencer and Tom Shenk of Spencer, Shenk, Capers Inc. in Gardena, California, and Dr. Nate Regier of Next Element Consulting in Newton, Kansas for introducing us to the leaders of some of their client companies and for encouraging those leaders to tell their stories.

We especially want to thank Dr. Franklin Schargel, the former president of the Education Division of the American Society for Quality (ASQ), to whom this book is dedicated. Franklin heard us present at a national dropout prevention conference, recognized the impact the concepts of Process Communication could have on education, and invited us to present at a conference he was running for the Education Division of ASQ. In fact, he said the concepts were "on the cutting edge." Since then, he has shared his philosophy of leadership and quality with us and has been a close friend and advisor.

Most of all we are indebted to Dr. Taibi Kahler, the clinical psychologist who made the discoveries on which the concepts of Process Communication are based. For more than 38 years, Dr. Kahler's discoveries have been enriching the lives of people in all walks of life and we have enjoyed our association with him for more than 23 years. He changed our leadership style and his Process Communication Model® enabled us to be more effective leaders in every organization we have headed. More importantly, the concepts of Process Communication have enabled us to improve the lives of all those with whom we interact every day and have enabled us to have a significant impact on teachers, students, and educational leaders throughout the country. Thank you, Taibi.

Finally, we want to thank the people at ASQ and Sorensen Publishing, especially Matt Meinholz, Paul O'Mara, Randy Benson, Janet Sorensen, and Linda Presto for their help in producing this book. This is a better book because of their professionalism, competence, and commitment. They set deadlines and met them. More importantly, they helped us meet ours. It has been a pleasure working with them.

Introduction

Now you are a leader. Your board of directors expects you to lead the company or organization to increased performance and profitability. You have a vision of where you want to go and how you want to get there. The task now is to get your employees to see your vision and to march with you in lock step to accomplish it. To succeed, you must get them to want to follow you. To do that you must be able to communicate your vision clearly and concisely so that everyone sees the vision and sees that accomplishing it is to their advantage. The purpose of this book is to help you communicate more effectively so that you can motivate every employee to want to carry out your vision.

The concepts described in this book are scientifically based and have withstood more than 38 years of scrutiny and scientific inquiry. They first were used as a clinical model to help patients help themselves. Indeed, they still are used clinically. The originator of the concepts, Dr. Taibi Kahler, is an internationally recognized clinical psychologist who was awarded the 1977 Eric Berne Memorial Scientific Award for the clinical application of a discovery he made in 1971. That discovery enabled clinicians to shorten significantly the treatment time of patients by reducing their resistance as a result of miscommunication between their doctors and themselves.

Dr. Terrance McGuire, the consulting psychiatrist for the space program at NASA for more than 40 years, was so impressed by Dr. Kahler that he invited Dr. Kahler to participate in the 1978 round of astronaut selection interviews. Because of his involvement with the space program, Dr. Kahler turned the concepts into a behavioral model. CEOs heard of the concepts and began asking Dr. Kahler to translate the model into management terms. In 1981 Dr. Kahler developed a commercial model that is used today in corporations and other organizations all over the world to increase employee productivity, job satisfaction, morale, and corporate profitability. Since 1986 the model has also been used in education to help teachers individualize instruction in order to reach and teach every student more effectively.

The concepts are universal, that is, they apply in every culture. They have proven effective everywhere they are used—in the United States, Canada, Europe, Asia, Australia, New Zealand, Africa, Latin America, and the Caribbean. CEOs have said that they would hate to have to run their companies without the benefit of these tools. President Bill Clinton told the authors in 1997 that he considered Dr. Kahler to be a genius. He used the concepts in his speeches and used Dr. Kahler as a psycho-demographer during his presidency.

One of the authors, Joe Pauley, first learned of the concepts as a management tool when working for the U.S. government. He used the concepts to increase productivity and employee and customer satisfaction in every department he headed. For the past 21 years he has used the concepts in leading a successful consulting company and in helping leaders in the private sector, in government, in non-profits, and in education improve the productivity and profitability of their organizations. The other author, Judy Pauley, used the concepts in leading the science department of a high school where she taught chemistry and physics, in leading several scientific organizations, and in inspiring her chemistry and physics students to pursue careers in various science and engineering fields. She was named Science Teacher of the Year three times. For the past 15 years she successfully led her company in helping educators reach and teach every student. The Pauleys are the recipients of the 2008 Individual Crystal Star Award from the National Dropout Prevention Network at Clemson University for their work in helping educators apply the concepts in their classrooms to reach and teach every student and prepare them for work in the twenty-first century.

Enjoy the book.

1

Everyone is a Leader to Someone

"Leadership is a relationship between those who aspire to lead and those who choose to follow."

Jim Kouzes and Barry Posner, *A Leader's Legacy*

Leadership is all about relationships. When people think of leaders, they usually think of corporate CEOs, presidents of organizations, heads of state, senior military personnel, and people in similar positions. These people certainly are leaders. However, we think that everyone is a leader to someone—spouses to each other, parents to children, grandparents to grandchildren, teachers to students, clergy to their parishioners, managers to their staff, and so on. What all leaders need are followers. The following stories illustrate how three very different people applied the concepts of Dr. Taibi Kahler's Process Communication Model® to lead the people who followed them with great success in widely different circumstances.

LEADING A TURNAROUND SITUATION

Fred LeFranc is a turnaround specialist who has 30 years experience working in the restaurant chain business. He took over as CEO of a restaurant chain that was in trouble and turned it around using the concepts in this book. He was so successful that Inc. magazine did an article on him. He believes that understanding the concepts of Process Communication gives leaders a spotlight on someone's brain. This enables the leaders to understand where their team members are coming from, to be more tolerant of their positions, and to understand how to deal with them. He used the concepts in his strategic planning meetings and found that it took all of the noise out of meetings. It reduced the in-fighting and distress reactions and allowed his staff and restaurant managers to focus on improving the profitability of their restaurants. He believes that to be successful in turning a business around, CEOs must change the language and the culture of the business. The concepts of Process Communication explained in this book enabled him to do this very successfully.

Prior to this he was president of another company where he introduced the concepts of Process Communication and saw a 35 percent increase in same-store sales in three years. This was unheard of in the restaurant business. He also had double-digit growth in transaction average and in head count.

What did he do? He put his senior team through Process Communication training. They earned respect for each other and they learned to understand where everyone was coming from. They substituted knowledge of who they are for what they are. This led to everyone being more understanding and tolerant of each other and their problems and solutions.

His strategic plan was a living document that they referred to all the time. They met every two weeks as a team and discussed strategic goals and tactical goals using the strategic plan document as a guide. The concepts of Process Communication provided the communication strategies.

When he took over the company, meetings were unproductive. Some people preached at their colleagues, others criticized people for not paying attention to data. Still others made mistakes and complained that the company was not concerned about people. Several others made jokes and did things to irritate everyone else.

After being trained in the concepts of Process Communication, the team understood what was behind the statements and behaviors of the other team members and they became a cohesive force. When someone preached, the others said, "Okay, that's the way he is." They would shut up and let people talk instead of doing something to make them angrier. When people made a joke to lighten things up, the others understood and did not take offense. Everyone accepted the behaviors of the other team members and maintained their focus on improving the profitability of their restaurants. As a result, meetings were shorter and much more productive and the company prospered.

Fred believed it was crucial that everyone on the team understand each other and each other's role in the company and he used the concepts of Process Communication to accomplish this. He also used two demonstrations to illustrate why they needed to function as a team. He assembled 20 people in a room and asked them each to think of a game to play with a ball. They came up with several different games. He then had them start to play the game. What are the rules of the game? They quickly realized they were playing by different rules. There was no cohesion. "Welcome to the business world and to our company. If we each play by different rules we are not going to succeed. In sports, everyone on a team knows the rules of their sport and their role on the team. Everyone knows what the team goal is and knows everyone else's role on the team. They all know all the stats. They are effective. If we are to be effective, we must do the same thing." The concepts of Process Communication were the guiding spirit for the understanding.

He asked them two questions. Is the organization smart? Is the organization healthy? He believed the company had to be both in order to succeed. To illustrate this he had the team members stand around a table that held cups of tea. He asked half the group to watch from one side of the table while the other half attempted to lift the table without spilling any tea. They could not do it. Then he had the other half try. They could not do it either. Finally, he asked them all to put two fingers under the table and all lift together on the count of three. The table easily rose two feet into the air. They were amazed at how easy it was to raise the table without spilling the tea when they all worked together.

Fred helped his managers get their psychological needs met every day and made sure that his managers helped their employees get their needs met as well. As a result, quality and morale were high, turnover was low, and service and profitability soared.

LEADING A REORGANIZATION

Paul was the Vice President in charge of collections in one of the largest financial institutions in the world. When he took over his new division, morale was low and there were invisible walls built up between the different departments. People from one department did not talk to people from the other departments and, as a result, there were repetitive emails to customers, contentious phone calls to customers, and contentious phone calls and emails between employees in different sections of the division.

Paul heard about the concepts of Process Communication and decided that he could use them to communicate more effectively with his staff and build trust with them. He believed this was crucial if he wanted to reduce tension and improve the performance of everyone in the division. Paul intended to combine the different departments in an effort to break down the walls that existed between them. For that to work, they needed a common language. When Paul had everyone in the division trained in the concepts of Process Communication, the result was an exponential increase in trust and in relationships between employees. They began to communicate with each other more effectively and to resolve issues with each other and with their customers. They began talking about things other than work and they began to trust him. They began to buy in to his plans. He communicated his trust to the managers and they in turn communicated their trust to their people. The performance improvement was quantifiable. They contributed an additional $10 million to the company's profit the following year.

His people also improved their performance. They learned how to assess the personality type of a customer within the first few sentences of a phone conversation. They then shifted to the customer's frame of reference for the rest of the communication. When customers were in distress they frequently were able to invite them out of distress very quickly and effectively. As a result, they solved problems faster and there were fewer repeat phone calls. With increased success, the morale of all of his staff gradually improved.

Paul also benefited personally. He now has a different view of the various personalities of his staff members. He understands their strengths and where they are coming from and this makes him more tolerant of their differences. In brainstorming sessions he plays to their strengths and encourages a more creative environment. He ensures that every meeting includes someone who is light-hearted and fun to keep the session light and to provide creative ideas. He also has someone in the group who is concerned about people to make sure he does not lose his focus on people. He always has someone in the group who is good at analyzing problems and who works well with data to make sure they stay on task. After a brainstorming session he invariably gets an email from someone who needs extra time to process information and make suggestions. The email always begins, "Oh, by the way, I was also thinking about...."

His people work in a high-intensity, high-pressure environment. He makes certain that they get their psychological needs met so that they stay in a positive place and do not get into distress.

As a result of the training, Paul is much more conscious of himself and how he comes across to other people. He also realizes that it is not about him. It is not about what makes him comfortable, but what makes his people comfortable. In his personal life he and his wife used to argue about financial matters all the time. Now he realizes it was not about the finances. It was about him not meeting the needs of his wife, who is very different from him. Now that he understands, he makes sure his wife gets her needs met every day. They still disagree on things, but they no longer have arguments. This has improved the situation at home significantly. As a result, he comes to work in a better frame of mind every day and is better able to meet the needs of his staff.

When he first introduced the training to his staff, their initial reaction was to ask why they had to shift to the other person's frame of reference. "Let them come to me." They don't say that anymore because they have seen how much more successful they are and how much happier they are with their jobs. They work more effectively as a team because they understand each other's strengths and frame of reference. They use a common language in communicating with each other. Paul recently had a brainstorming meeting about a complex and complete process change. He stated that he would not have considered having the session without being able to use the concepts that are contained in this book.

LEADING IN EDUCATION

Jennifer Sheehey teaches in a middle school (grades 6-8) in a suburban neighborhood in southern California. It had been the lowest performing middle school in the district on standardized testing for several years.

The school recently began the practice of co-teaching and fully mainstreaming all of the students in the Resource Program into the general education setting, including the students in Jennifer's class. There were 31 seventh grade students, a mixture of "lower performing" students and students with special needs. There were two teachers in the classroom—a Resource Specialist and a General Education Language Arts teacher who co-taught and co-planned all daily lessons.

The students in this class were "infamous" with the administration and other teachers on campus because they were constantly in trouble for fights, classroom disruption, stealing, and swearing at teachers. Because they did not act this way in their Language Arts class, Jennifer was inspired to undertake this research project.

Jennifer decided to examine why these students acted differently in some classes than others, and specifically wanted to see whether the students preferred one teacher's communication style to that of other teachers. She decided to tell the students about the concepts of Process Communication. In the process of learning about the various personality types and the needs of each, they began asking for more information. Specifically, they wanted to know how they could communicate better with their teachers. Jennifer saw this as an opportunity to lead her students to develop a positive attitude toward school and improve their lives. In this way she led them to empower themselves using some of the concepts of Process Communication. She decided to expand her research to see whether teaching students how to get their needs met positively would increase their academic achievement and result in their improving their behaviors in the classroom and on campus.

After having the students identify their own individual types, she explained what their needs were and she helped them work out positive ways to get those needs met. These are the results:

- Sixteen students raised their GPA and five students maintained their current average!

- Ten students had slightly lower GPAs but showed a huge turn around in behavior.

- Six had no discipline incidents for the remainder of the year.

- Three students significantly lowered the number of discipline incidents.

One student in particular was about to be expelled from school at the time Jennifer decided to tell them about Process Communication. He had accumulated 15 recorded discipline incidents during the year. After he learned how to get his needs met positively, he had no more discipline incidents. At the end of the year the student told her that he now knew how to get his needs met without fighting and he found it much easier to talk to his teachers. He did not get expelled. He is still in school and he loves the eighth grade.

Before being told about Process Communication, only 17 students in the class had not been in trouble during the school year. After learning about Process Communication, *23 students were able to stay out of trouble.* Before learning about Process Communication, there were 28 recorded referrals for disruption/defiance in the classroom and 12 fights. After learning about Process Communication, there were only *two referrals for disruption or defiance in class and two fights.* The students learned how to communicate instead of acting out as a means of getting their needs met.

After being told about the concepts of Process Communication, two female students separately approached their teacher to confess that they were cutting themselves and had thought about committing suicide. They said they needed help and wanted to talk to someone instead of hurting themselves again. They both entered counseling and report that they haven't cut themselves or had suicidal thoughts since. The concepts of Process Communication made it possible to open these lines of communication and make the students feel safe to come forward.

Overall, 30 of 31 students showed either an academic or behavioral turn around after being told about Process Communication!

The students wrote letters to the teachers they would have the next year, telling them about their personality types and their needs. In the letter they asked the teachers to help them get their needs met in class so they could learn more. The eighth grade teachers asked Jennifer for help in understanding how they could do this. The students now are in the eighth grade. Their entire attitude toward school has changed and they no longer talk about dropping out when they turn 16. Jennifer not only led the students to change their outlooks and behaviors, but very quietly influenced the other teachers to help their students get their motivational needs met positively by individualizing the way they teach.

By now, readers probably are wondering what the concepts of Process Communication are. They are explained in detail in the following chapters with additional examples. All of the stories in this book are true. Because many of the stories discuss turning negative situations into positive ones, we have eliminated the names of many of the companies and organizations, and in some cases have changed the name of the leaders.

2

Organizing the Team

"Leadership is the art of getting someone else to do what you want done because they want to do it."

President Dwight D. Eisenhower

What is a leader and what does a leader do? According to Eisenhower, leaders must be able to persuade others to help carry out their vision of the future. To accomplish this, the leader must have many talents. Other books have talked about some of these talents, including integrity, honesty, vision, responsibility, and the ability to establish relationships, listen, influence others, establish trust, develop leaders, develop the strengths of all employees, and communicate effectively, to name a few. Lee Iacocca, the former CEO of Chrysler Corporation, lists nine traits that every leader must have in his book *Where Have all the Leaders Gone?* These are the traits that leaders should be judged against. He called them the 9 Cs: Curiosity, Creativity, Character, Courage, Conviction, Charisma, Competence, Common Sense, and the ability to Communicate.

Everyone says that a leader must be able to communicate; however, none of the leadership books tells the leader how to communicate effectively so that every stakeholder sees the vision, understands why it is a desirable goal, and buys into the steps necessary to achieve it. It is imperative that the leader has a vision. It is critical that he or she has the ability to communicate the vision to every stake holder—to the board of directors, to her or his direct reports, to every manager, to every employee in the organization, to stockholders, to clients, to the media, and to the public. We will explain how to do this in this chapter and in Chapter 3 and Chapter 4. Throughout the book we will give examples of how leaders have successfully used the concepts in leading their organizations.

The ability to communicate is more than the ability to stand before an audience and make a speech or to talk one on one with individuals. Leaders must ensure that everyone sees the vision and is working every day to help achieve it. People must be placed in positions where they are able to do what they do best every day. They must know what is expected of them, and they must be committed to doing quality work. They must have the tools to do their jobs well, they must believe their jobs are important, they must feel valued by the organization, and they must get their motivational needs met every day.

Many of these factors are obvious and easily accomplished. Less obvious and less easily accomplished are individualizing communication and ensuring that every employee gets her or his needs met every day. To understand these needs, let's look at Dr. Taibi Kahler's Process Communication Model.® Dr. Kahler identified six different personality types based on how people take in and process information, that is, how they perceive the world. He called them Reactors, Workaholics, Persisters, Dreamers, Rebels, and Promoters.

Reactors are people who feel first. They feel the texture of their clothes and the food they eat, and they relate to people and things in the world around them by how they feel about them. They are compassionate, sensitive, and warm, and they have great interpersonal skills. Their goal in life is to help everyone to feel good. They prefer to work with groups of people they feel comfortable with.

Workaholics, on the other hand, are goal-oriented self-starters who thrive on data. They are responsible, logical, and organized, and they perceive the world through their thoughts. They think first and want others to think with them. Because they are goal oriented and think clearly, they expect others to be goal oriented and able to think clearly too.

Persisters have a strongly developed sense of right and wrong and judge everyone according to their value system. In fact, values are their currency and they expect others to have high standards and values too. They are conscientious, dedicated, and observant and, like the Workaholic, they are goal oriented. They form opinions very quickly and are quick to act on them. They are driven to succeed; because of their commitment and determination, they frequently rise to leadership positions in an organization. One of their strengths is their ability to stick to a task they believe in until they accomplish it.

Dreamers are people who are very different from the other five types. They are reflective, imaginative, and calm, and they see the world very differently from the others. They need time to reflect on tasks and topics before they contribute to a discussion or take an action. When given time to reflect, they frequently are very insightful and they make observations that the other types have not thought about. They head the list of those who think outside the box; however, they must be given time to reflect on topics before being expected to contribute their ideas.

Rebels are our most creative employees. They react to people and things with likes and dislikes, and they can have wide mood swings. They can go from love to hate in a nanosecond. They like to have fun and can best be described as people who are creative, spontaneous, and playful. They are free spirits and thrive in an environment that encourages their creativity and allows them freedom to express their individuality and playfulness.

Promoters are natural entrepreneurs. They are action oriented and thrive on challenges and excitement. They are persuasive, adaptable, and charming, and they love to sell. They live on the edge and respond best to short-term challenges and quick rewards. They are natural leaders; because of their persuasiveness and willingness to take risks, many Promoters become leaders of start-up companies or sales departments.

Although everyone is one of these six types, each person has parts of all six in them; some parts are used more often than others. Dr. Kahler describes this as a six-floor condominium with the strongest part as the base and the other parts in ascending order of dominance. Figure 2.1 is the profile of a typical Fortune 500 CEO. As a base Persister, this leader is conscientious, dedicated, and observant. With Workaholic second and well developed in her or his personality structure, he or she also is organized, responsible, and logical and able to think clearly. Note that Promoter is third and also well developed. This leader is action oriented and willing to take risks to achieve goals.

Let's look at the impact of the different personality structures from the point of view of the leader in Figure 2.1 and from that of an employee who is quite different from the leader. According to Dr. Kahler, employees who are like the leader in Figure 2.1 will hear his messages and understand what is expected of them. Employees who are not like the leader, for example the

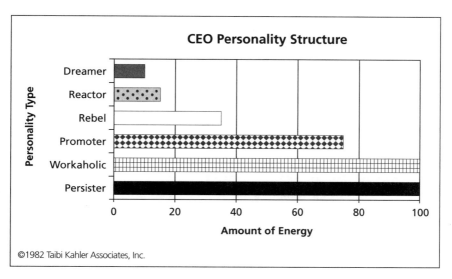

Figure 2.1 Typical Fortune 500 CEO.

employee with a personality structure like that in Figure 2.2, will not hear and understand unless the leader individualizes the way he or she communicates and motivates all of her or his direct reports. This is because each of the six types is motivated differently, communicates differently, prefers a different management style, learns differently, and does different things when in distress. We will discuss each of these in subsequent chapters. For now, let's look at the personality structure of the employee in Figure 2.2 and compare it with that of the leader in Figure 2.1.

This employee is a Reactor and could be either male or female. For the purposes of this example, we will assume the employee is female. She is compassionate, sensitive, and warm, and feels first. This employee is people oriented, has great people skills, and genuinely cares how people feel; she wants everyone to feel good. Completion of tasks is less important to her than working with people with whom she feels comfortable and having people like her. She has Rebel on the second floor of her condominium. Therefore, she has a lot of creativity and likes to have fun. Dreamer is her next most well-developed part. Therefore, she has some ability to conceptualize and see connections between things that others may not see. Workaholic is on her fourth floor and is not very well developed. Therefore, she has some ability to be logical and to think clearly, but this is not her strong suit. She is not particularly task oriented. Persister is on the fifth floor of her condominium and is an even less well-developed part of her personality structure. As a result, she does not have strongly held opinions. In fact, in elections she normally votes for candidates she feels are nice people and does not necessarily vote on the issues. Promoter is the least

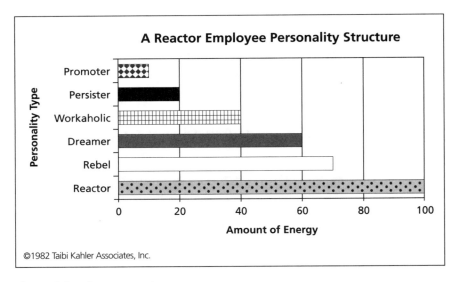

Figure 2.2   Reactor employee.

well-developed part of her personality. She is not adventuresome and does not feel comfortable taking risks. She is most comfortable keeping her savings in certificates of deposit or savings accounts. If she invests in the stock market, she normally will invest in ultra conservative stocks.

Most adults can energize two or three of their personality parts very easily. Most children can energize only one or two. Therein lies the problem. The leader in Figure 2.1 energizes his Persister part most often and he energizes his Workaholic part very easily. He also uses his Promoter part quite often and wants to get things done. He rarely ever uses the Dreamer or Reactor parts of his personality. His personality structure is almost the reverse of the employee in Figure 2.2. As a result, the employee in Figure 2.2 may feel that the leader does not like her. She probably will get into distress about it and will not hear the leader's message, see the leader's vision, or understand what is expected of her to help carry it out.

What can the leader do about it? The rest of this book answers that question. Because each of the six types has different strengths, all have something to contribute to the organization in helping to carry out the leader's vision. Wise leaders assess the character strengths needed to achieve their vision and deliberately seek out those persons who have the strengths needed. We saw this in the examples in the previous chapter. Fred LeFranc, the turnaround specialist, always ensured that there was at least one Rebel, one Promoter, one Workaholic, one Persister, one Reactor, and one Dreamer in every meeting to guarantee that issues would be examined from every angle and every viewpoint would be represented. However, because each of the personality types is different, the leader must use different strategies to make certain that everyone has an opportunity to provide input.

For example, the strategic planning group in a California high-tech company consisted of six people. There were three Persisters, two Workaholics, and one Dreamer named Mary. Mary was an intelligent Stanford Law School graduate who was by nature very quiet and not at all competitive. The other members of the team completely dominated the meetings. They were smart and extremely fast, qualities they believed indicated their intelligence, and Mary rarely opened her mouth. She wasn't seen as adding much of value and they believed she was too slow. After one meeting, the president of the company, who knew her to be smart and thoughtful, asked her why she never said anything at the meetings. She replied, "Too many chiefs." She added that she wasn't certain anyone wanted to hear her.

The president assured her that he wanted her input and directed her to express her ideas. Her analysis and suggestions were far superior to many that were offered by the other team members. The team, after recovering from their shock, adopted her suggestion and implemented her strategy and the company profited. After others learned how she thought about and processed information, she was swamped with requests to join various teams. Over the next three months Mary was out for 14 sick days because of stress and pressure. She requested that she be allowed to operate on the sidelines with these various groups and provide her input in writing. This was a win for everyone and Mary was out for only two sick days over the next three years. From then on, the president made sure he took time after every meeting to ask for her input privately. Frequently her solutions to problems were outside the box, but they usually were more effective than those proposed by other team members. Because it was a cohesive team, the other team members soon began asking for her input on everything.

Successful leaders recognize the talents of all their employees and know how to gain access to those talents. However, to do this successfully, they must be able to communicate with and motivate each person individually. We will explain how to do this in the following chapters.

3

Establishing Trust

"A company is an organic, living, breathing thing, not just an income sheet and balance sheet. You have to lead it with that in mind. "

Carleton S. Fiorina
former CEO of Hewlett-Packard

Webster's dictionary defines *trust* as "to place confidence in, to rely on." Each of the six personality types interprets this differently based on individual perceptions of the world. For example, Persisters believe they can trust leaders who keep their word and maintain confidences, and who are committed to high morals, high standards, and high quality work. Reactors feel that they can have confidence in leaders who demonstrate that they care about the well being of the people in an organization as well as clients and customers. Workaholics trust leaders who are fair, who think clearly and logically, who appreciate those who work hard and are able to analyze situations carefully, and who are willing to consider various options for moving the organization forward.

Dreamers trust leaders who are direct with them, who understand that they need time to reflect on problems and various courses of action, and who appreciate their unique insights into people and problems. Rebels like leaders who are fun to work for and who encourage their creativity. They trust leaders who allow them to say what they like and don't like without fear of recriminations and who give them freedom in the way they do their work. Promoters trust leaders who are action oriented and decisive, leaders who make things happen and who give them challenges to work on and opportunities to look good.

This, then, is the key for leaders who want to establish trust with each of the six personality types: have integrity, walk the talk, mean what you say and say what you mean, be direct, care about people, be fair, work hard, trust your employees, be decisive, be fun to work for, and appreciate the unique contributions of each individual. Communication is the key to demonstrating all of these qualities and earning the trust of every employee.

As noted in Chapter 2, each of the six personality types communicates differently. This means that there are six different versions of every language. For example, if everyone speaks a common language, say English, there are six distinct versions based on the perceptions of the six types. They are so different that they may be considered separate languages. A leader who wants to reach all of her or his employees must speak all six of these languages at some time. It is similar to traveling to a foreign country, for example China. If the leader wants to go to China and the people do not speak English, the leader must be able to speak Chinese if he or she wants to be understood. The leader might use an interpreter, but in that case the leader is dependent on the competence, understanding, and integrity of the interpreter to be certain that his message is being accurately conveyed, correctly interpreted, and completely understood. Learning six versions of a common language may seem to be a daunting task. Fortunately, it is not. This chapter will provide the framework for leaders who will be able to use all six languages whenever they want to. There are two aspects of this. The first is "the language of perceptions." The second is the preferred "channel of communication" of each of the types.

THE LANGUAGE OF PERCEPTIONS

As noted in Chapter 2, each of the six types perceives the world differently. Reactors perceive the world through their emotions. They take in people and things through feeling for and about them. They want to share their feelings with others and they want others to share their feelings with them. Workaholics, on the other hand, perceive the world through thoughts. They are data oriented and seek information. They want to share their information and they want people to think with them.

Workaholics and Reactors often marry each other and friction results in the marriage because they speak different versions of a common language. The Reactor spouse (for example, the wife) wants the Workaholic spouse to feel with her and the Workaholic spouse wants the Reactor to think with him. They perceive the world differently and speak different languages.

Persisters perceive the world through their opinions. When they get information, they very quickly form a value judgment. They have an opinion about nearly everything and expect people to ask their opinions about things. They tend to marry Reactors or Workaholics and friction results from the different perceptions of the world around them and the different languages they speak.

Dreamers perceive the world through inaction or reflection. They tend to reflect on subjects before speaking and are often slow and deliberate when they do speak. They tend not to undertake a task until someone tells them to do so.

Rebels perceive the world through their reactions. They let everyone know what they like and what they do not like, usually without regard to the consequences.

Promoters perceive the world through action. They act first, usually without thinking about the consequences of their actions. They want people to act with them and they get impatient when people engage in prolonged discussions. They want information succinctly and in bullets.

It is easy to see how friction arises in marriages between all of these types based on their perceptions of the world and the languages they speak. The same frictions arise in the workplace between the different types. For example, a Promoter leader in an entertainment company in California was action oriented. He was very knowledgeable and had a lot of experience. Much of his communication moved at the speed of light. His direct reports perceived the world through thoughts. They wanted time to think things through and be more client oriented. He wanted them to think like he did, make quick decisions, and come to the table prepared to discuss issues. He thought he was hauling them along and they thought he was pushing them. When he learned about the perceptions of the different personality types, he understood the reason for the miscommunication and began to give them 24 hours to research an issue and think it through. They then would come back to him with proposed solutions or courses of action. Within two months the staff members were able to reach solutions faster than the allotted 24 hours and were giving him the information he needed much faster. Both sides ended up giving a little and everyone benefited.

One thing that can help leaders identify the perception and personality types of people with whom they want to communicate is to listen to the words they use in communicating with others. Because people also use the perceptions they are most comfortable with in their writing, leaders also can look at their written material.

As we saw, Reactors speak the language of Emotions. A Reactor officer in one government agency used this language in writing guidance papers for subordinate offices around the country. She always told them how wonderful they were instead of focusing on the subject on which she was providing guidance. When she did provide guidance, she preceded her guidance with "I feel that...." Her Persister boss spoke the language of Opinions. He repeatedly told her to stop telling people how wonderful they were and concentrate on providing guidance. He usually added, "I believe you should tell them your opinion of what they proposed doing." The officer usually responded by telling her boss how she felt. As their relationship deteriorated, she started having automobile accidents. After learning about the different perceptions, the boss understood why she spoke and wrote as she did and he began speaking the language of

Emotions with her. He began asking her how she felt about things instead of asking her opinion of things. As a result, her morale improved and she stopped having accidents.

Percy Thomas, the former Provost of the Continuing Education Department at Montgomery College in Maryland, is a Persister. His wife is a Reactor and they have a granddaughter who is a Rebel. The fact that the Rebel granddaughter was leaving her clothes all over the house bothered Percy and his wife. In an effort to get the granddaughter to pick up her things, the wife spoke to her using her favorite language, the language of Emotions. The granddaughter ignored her and did not pick up her clothes. Although Percy is most comfortable speaking the language of Opinions in communicating with people, he decided he would speak the language of Reactions to try to get his granddaughter to pick up her things. He took her clothes and threw them all over the stairs. He pretended to be the clothes and called to the granddaughter, telling her that they wanted to be put away. The granddaughter laughed, picked up all the clothes, and put them away. She then said to Percy in the language of Reactions, "I like it when you speak to me like that, Grandpa. You speak my language."

A Dreamer employee of an agency of the United States government was very slow and deliberate in doing everything. She almost always spoke the language of Inaction and asked for more time to reflect on subjects before she said or did anything. Her Workaholic boss was highly critical of her because she took so much time. The Workaholic boss always spoke to her using the language of Thoughts, saying things such as "What work have you done today?" The Dreamer frequently responded, "I don't know." If the boss asked why she wasn't more assertive in making certain others met their deadlines, the Dreamer frequently said things such as "I didn't want to rock the boat." This almost always resulted in harsh criticism. As a result, their relationship deteriorated until the Dreamer got sick and missed several weeks of work. After the boss learned about the languages of perceptions, he began telling her to do one thing at a time. For example, he might say, "Tell me one thing you did in the office today." This always resulted in a crisp response, indicating that the Dreamer was comfortable speaking that language.

A Workaholic leader of a Fortune 100 company was running a meeting. He was speaking the language of Thoughts and asking for suggestions and information from the other attendees. He asked what their options were and then talked about time frames to accomplish the various options. The meeting dragged on as everyone spoke the language of thoughts and gave more information. Finally, a Promoter leader from another part of the company shouted in the language of Action: "For God's sake, stop talking and do something. Make something happen." He then stomped out of the meeting. What might the Workaholic have said in the language of Action? "Tell us what you are going to do."

If leaders speak only the language of their favorite perception, they are inviting everyone into distress who is not comfortable with that language. Leaders who want to be effective communicators must individualize the way they speak to everyone. This is especially true if they want to persuade people to embrace a Quality program.

It is easy to speak these languages one on one, but can it be done in a group, for example while running meetings? Yes, it can, and without too much difficulty. The authors start every meeting we run like this: "I appreciate your being here on time. It shows that you care about each other. (Said in a soft tone.) We have a lot of important work to accomplish today. (Said in a matter-of-fact tone.) I sent you the items I have on my agenda so that you could reflect about them and be prepared to discuss them this morning. (Said slowly in a matter-of-fact tone.) If you have something you want to discuss, please let me know and we will decide where it goes on the agenda. (Said in a matter-of-fact tone.) We want to make sure we cover the most important items first. (Said in a matter-of-fact tone.) I figure it will take us about 45 minutes to cover all the items on the agenda. If we need more time, we can take it, but let's shoot for 45 minutes. Is that okay with everyone? (Said in a matter-of-fact tone.) Before we start, I'd like to share a funny story with you. (Said in an upbeat, energetic way.) Okay, let's get those creative juices flowing and generate some great action ideas. Let's get to it." (Said with energy.)

In this way, everyone hears the entire opening message and everyone gets a "battery charge" at their part of it. Throughout the rest of the meeting we alternate using the various languages to keep everyone tuned in and interested in what we are talking about. Does this work? Absolutely! In fact, this is how elections are won and lost.

Several elections ago Governor Dukakis of Massachusetts was running for President against George H. W. Bush. According to the polls, he was leading Bush by 15 percentage points going into the first debate. During the debate the moderator, Bernard Shaw, asked Governor Dukakis this question. "Governor, you have said that you are opposed to the death penalty in the case of rape. If Kitty Dukakis were raped and murdered, would you favor an irrevocable death penalty for the killer?" Governor Dukakis answered the question factually, using only the language of Persisters and Workaholics. The moderator then asked the same question of George Bush. He replied in the language of Reactors. He softened his tone and said, "Oh Bernie, how can you even ask such a question?" That was the turning point in the election. The polls the next morning had George Bush ahead by 15 percentage points—a 30-point swing. Coincidentally, Reactors make up 30 percent of the North American population. For the first time in the campaign, someone spoke their language and they responded. Throughout the rest of the campaign, Governor Dukakis never spoke their language and George Bush was elected President.

Four years later President Bush ran against Bill Clinton. When Clinton was the governor of Arkansas, Dr. Kahler ran a special seminar for him and a few of his friends. From then on Governor Clinton used these concepts in his speeches and in leading his administrations. He also used the concepts to get himself elected President and re-elected even when he was embroiled in a scandal that resulted in impeachment proceedings against him. During one of the debates in his re-election campaign against Senator Bob Dole, a woman in the audience asked Senator Dole a question about health care. Senator Dole responded factually using the language of Persisters and Workaholics. President Clinton assessed the woman as a Reactor. He came down off the stage, knelt beside her, and touched her on the arm. Using Reactor language he said, "I feel your pain." That was the turning point in the campaign. The Republicans recognized that it was a turning point and have included a provision in every debate agreement since then: the candidates agree that they will not leave the stage to go into the audience.

In their campaigns for President, Vice President Al Gore and Senator John Kerry spoke only the language of Persisters and Workaholics and lost. In her campaign for President, Senator Hillary Clinton was widely perceived to be the front-runner for the Democratic nomination. In her campaign, she spoke only the language of Persisters and Workaholics. This allowed Barack Obama, who spoke the language of several types, to mount a serious challenge to her for the Democratic nomination. In the final days of the primary campaign in New Hampshire, the polls indicated Senator Clinton was about to suffer a double-digit loss. She finally spoke the language of Reactors during the weekend before the election and, in an upset, won the primary. She failed to keep it up in subsequent primaries, however, and Senator Obama became the Democratic nominee. His opponent in the general election, Senator John McCain, spoke only the language of Persisters and Workaholics and fell behind in the polls. He began to speak with more energy in the last few days, but it was too little, too late, and Obama won the Presidency.

Unfortunately, few politicians speak the languages of Rebels or Dreamers. Rebels make up 20 percent of the population in North America, Dreamers make up 10 percent, and few vote regularly in elections. The leaders and managers in corporations, government agencies, and other organizations often don't speak the language of Rebels and Dreamers either. This lack of communication leads Rebels and Dreamers to be unhappy in their jobs and frequently results in friction between them and their managers and leaders. In a seminar the authors conducted several years ago, one of the participants, a Rebel, asked, "Why wouldn't everyone want to have Rebels working for them?" The former president of a major U.S. corporation immediately replied, "Because you never come to work on time; you don't follow the dress code; you wear sandals instead of shoes; you are late for meetings, and you don't follow instructions. However, we know we need you, so we put up with you." This friction is easily eliminated or greatly reduced when leaders and managers speak the language of each of the types and individualize the way they motivate people. If leaders want to lead successfully, they must speak the language of all the people they want to lead. Otherwise they will not be successful.

John Bishop, the CEO of Cepheid, a company that develops genetics-based analysis systems for clinical diagnosis and bio-threat assessment in Sunnyvale, California, keeps a piece of paper in his desk that contains bar graphs displaying the personality attributes of his key employees. He maintains that he holds the list more useful than anything else in his office because the bar graphs enable him to communicate more effectively with the individuals on his staff. He has found that by knowing how individuals on his staff approach the world, he can best understand how they approach problems and the likely basis for their recommendations and decisions.

For example, the Persisters on his staff make decisions based on the opinions they hold. The Reactors on his staff make decisions based on the impact they will have on people. His Rebels make decisions based on how creative the solution is or how much fun they will derive from a specific choice. The Promoters on his staff make decisions based on what may be the most expedient choice in a given situation or perhaps the choice that will give the most excitement or immediate reward. The Workaholics on his staff are goal oriented and approach the world by thinking about logical solutions. Because he knows how his staff thinks, he can both understand the motivations for their recommendations and communicate his positions to them in the way most likely to generate a response. He used this knowledge to achieve his goals of high-quality products, positive cash flow, and an increase in revenue from $85 million to $100 million per year.

The other part of individualizing communication is to use the preferred "channel" of each individual. These channels are described and their usage explained in Chapter 4.

4

Inspiring Confidence

"A true leader always strives to inspire."

Lee Iacocca,
former CEO of Chrysler Corporation

Many leaders say that the key to establishing trust is to communicate clearly with your employees and staff members. They talk about keeping everyone informed, saying what you mean and meaning what you say, and always telling the truth. They also talk about giving honest and complete feedback to staff members. As we saw in Chapter 3, communicating effectively is much more than that. It involves speaking in the other person's language and using his or her preferred channel of communication. This chapter describes the other aspect of communicating effectively—the concept of channels of communication.

Rose Wynne Brookes, the vice president for Strategy and Corporate Development in a major financial services company in the United States, was having a difficult time communicating with a rebel team member who was feeling frustrated working in a Persister/Workaholic environment. Rose Wynne changed the words she used and the tone of her voice to communicate with him in his preferred channel of communication. He became a team player and began contributing creative ideas to help the team advance her vision. She also used the appropriate channels in dealing with the other team members and the team became more productive as well. Rose Wynne also found that she listened more carefully. By using the preferred channel and perception of each of her team members, she was able to accomplish everything she wanted to in 15 minutes rather than in the hour she had scheduled for the meetings.

Sylvester Hopewell, the past president of the 100 Black Men of DeKalb County, Georgia, and the current chairman of their Education Committee, used channels and perceptions in dealing with the members of his executive board every day. Most were Promoters who were successful entrepreneurial businessmen. They wanted to help but they were busy and time was important to them. They repeatedly told Sylvester, "Just tell us what you want us to do and we'll do it." He did just that. He used their favorite channel and the perception of action, saying "Do this." They were happy that he spoke their language and they did what he wanted them to do. They were not interested in hearing the details of what was happening. Neither were they interested in hearing how people felt about what was happening. As long as Sylvester shifted to their frame of reference to communicate, they gladly did what he wanted them to do and the board functioned cohesively.

There are four channels preferred by the six personality types. (See Table 4.1.) These channels can be compared to the channels of a TV set or the stations on a radio. For example, if a leader is broadcasting on Channel 9 and an employee is watching for the broadcast on Channel 7, the employee will not hear the leader's message. A leader who wants to ensure that the message is heard must broadcast on the channel the employee is watching.

Another analogy features a room with four doors. Let's assume that the employee has a favorite door. When someone knocks on that door, he or she hears the knocking and responds. Let's also assume that the employee has one door that has been boarded up and two doors that he or she uses only occasionally. The employee never hears anyone knocking on the door that's boarded up. Now let's assume that particular door is a favorite of the leader. If the leader only knocks on the leader's favorite door, the employee will not hear the message and will not clearly understand what is expected of her or him. If someone knocks on the two doors that the employee uses only occasionally, the employee will understand the message some of the time and will not hear it at other times. Leaders who want their employees to hear their message must knock on the favorite door of each employee.

What are these channels and which ones work best with which types?

1. The *Directive* channel lets the listener know exactly what is expected and is given as a clear command. For example, "Tell me

Table 4.1 Channels of communication.

Type	Channel
Reactor	Nurturative
Workaholic	Requestive
Persister	Requestive
Dreamer	Directive
Rebel	Emotive
Promoter	Directive

©1982 Taibi Kahler Associates, Inc.

where you are from." It is said in a matter-of-fact way without attacking or criticizing the other person. This channel works best with Promoters who need to know the bottom line and with Dreamers who tend not to undertake an action until being given clear direction to do something. It does not work well with Reactors, Workaholics, and Persisters; if used with Rebels, it may result in the Rebels doing the opposite of what they have been ordered to do.

2. The *Requestive* channel is used to ask for or give information. Persisters and Workaholics respond best to this channel. These personality types are self-motivated and usually know what is expected of them. Consequently, they prefer to be asked questions. For example, "Where are you from?" This is said matter-of-factly and not in a way that can be interpreted as an attack or criticism. Some leaders assume that everyone is open to this channel, but there are people who feel uncomfortable because it seems to them as if they are being grilled when asked a lot of questions. A former staff member of one of the authors is one of them. One day when talking with the authors about the various channels, she suddenly said, "Now I know why I hate to come to your office. All you ever do is grill me." We immediately changed the way we communicated with her.

3. The *Nurturative* channel is used to communicate with Reactors who prefer soft soothing tones and gentleness. People who do not have Reactor well developed in their personality structure are not comfortable with this channel and may reject it or misinterpret what is said. An example of this channel is: "That is a beautiful suit you are wearing." A simple "Thank you" indicates the person is comfortable with that channel. A "Same suit I've been wearing all week" response indicates that the person is not.

4. The *Emotive* channel is best to use with Rebels. This is a fun channel, and the speaker's tone is upbeat and energetic and may ring with enthusiasm. People using this channel frequently use slang in speaking to each other. For example, "Hey bro, that is one awesome suit, man." Unfortunately for Rebels, many people, especially Persisters and Workaholics who may be their bosses, are not comfortable with this channel and do not use it often, if at all. The result is often miscommunication between Rebel employees and their bosses.

In order for successful communication to take place between two people, there must be an offer and a prompt, clear response that makes sense. Table 4.2 lists the four channels and gives examples of what is and what is not clear, crisp communication. When leaders offer communication in one channel and get the kind of response listed in the miscommunication column, the subconscious message to the leader is, "I am not comfortable with that channel. Please use another channel." It is better if leaders use the correct channel every time, but when they use a channel with which the listener is not comfortable, they can listen to the response and offer a different channel, if necessary. People almost always get a second chance when communication does not take place the first time. When leaders listen to how people respond when they initiate communication in a channel, they will know whether or not communication is taking place.

ESTABLISHING CONTACT

To establish contact and communicate effectively, leaders should combine the appropriate perception with the preferred channel of the person with whom they are talking. (See Table 4.3.) In communicating with Workaholics,

Table 4.2 Communication and miscommunication.

Channel	Communication	Miscommunication
Directive	Tell me where the books are. In the back office.	Do you want me to tell you where the books are?
Requestive	Where are the books? In the back office.	Do you want me to tell you where the books are?
Nurturative	You always look so stylish. Thank you.	Same suit I've worn all week.
Emotive	I dig that crazy tie. Yeh, neat huh?	There's nothing wrong with my tie.

©1982 Taibi Kahler Associates, Inc.

Table 4.3 Perception and channel.

Type	Perception	Channel
Reactor	Emotions (Feelings)	Nurturative
Workaholic	Thoughts	Requestive
Persister	Opinions	Requestive
Dreamer	Inactions (Reflections)	Directive
Rebel	Reactions (Likes & Dislikes)	Emotive
Promoter	Actions	Directive

©1982 Taibi Kahler Associates, Inc.

leaders should use the Requestive channel and address the perception of thoughts. In other words, they should ask for information and data. For example, "What are our options?" or "What does the data show?" or "How much have you budgeted for this project?" Workaholics will immediately respond with the information requested. If leaders use a different channel or perception in speaking with a Workaholic, the employee may become confused and not able to answer the question. This explains what leaders mean when they say things such as, "I pull these levers, but what I want never happens; they must not be connected to anything." Or, "I must be speaking Chinese. I tell people what I want them to do, but they don't do it."

In communicating with Reactors, leaders should use the Nurturative channel and address the perception of emotions. For example, "Thank you for sharing your feelings about this with us." Or, "I appreciate your telling me how you feel about this new policy." Or, "Those earrings are very pretty." When people use a different channel or perception, if, for example, they ask for information or an opinion, Reactors may become confused and not know how to respond.

With Persisters, leaders should use the Requestive channel and ask for their opinions. For example, "What is your opinion of this?" Or, "What do you believe we should do?" With Rebels, leaders should use the Emotive channel and the perceptions of Reactions. For example, "Hey dude, that was an awesome report." Or, "Wow, look at that sunset. I love it." With Promoters, leaders should use the Directive channel and the perception of Actions. For example, "Tell me what you are going to do." Or, "Tell me what you did to land this contract."

Dreamers can only do one or two tasks at a time and normally don't undertake an action until they are told to do something. With Dreamers, leaders should use the Directive channel and tell them to do just one thing. For example, "Tell me one thing you are going to do to implement this new policy." Or, "Tell me one thing you did this morning."

When one of the authors, Joe, first learned of the concepts of Process Communication, he had a Dreamer secretary. She had great secretarial skills but was not getting any work done. He returned to the office from the seminar, identified her as a Dreamer, and used the Directive channel and the perception of Inaction with her. Overnight she became a highly productive employee. What did he do? Realizing that the secretary was a Dreamer and could only do one or two things at a time, he told her to tell him what she had pending and then he prioritized the list for her. The conversation went like this:

"Tell me what you have pending."

Answer, "Twenty-three things."

"Fine. First do this. Then do this. Then do this. When I give you something else to do, ask me where it goes on this list."

About two weeks later, the author's deputy, a Workaholic with Dreamer as the least well-developed part of her personality, said, "Wow, your secretary has really improved." The secretary always had great secretarial skills. The difference was that the author had learned how to communicate with her. The Directive channel is not the author's favorite channel and he had been of the opinion that employees should be able to do more than one thing at a time. This was a good lesson for him to accept people as they are, take advantage of their strengths, and find ways to help them overcome their weaknesses.

Channels of communication are also important when giving feedback to team members. Rebecca Amis, a school principal, was establishing an elementary school with her sister. One of the staff members was a Dreamer with Reactor as the second-strongest part of her personality. Whenever Rebecca wanted her to do something, she used the Directive channel. For example, the Dreamer arrived late to work every day. Rebecca used the Directive channel with her to get her to come to work on time. Because the Dreamer staff member had Reactor well developed, Rebecca also used the Nurturative channel with her occasionally, especially when giving her positive feedback. Another administrator was making mistakes because she felt she was not being heard. Rebecca used the Nurturative channel to tell her how much she was valued as a member of the staff. Her work improved significantly. Another administrator was a Promoter. Rebecca used the Directive channel with him and he responded well. When she used any other channel he would take over meetings and she would have to use the Directive channel to regain control. At first Rebecca was not comfortable individualizing the way she spoke with her team members and it took a lot of energy on her part. When she saw the results, she felt it was worth the effort because her staff members were so much more productive.

Leaders who want to inspire their employees to follow them and help them accomplish their vision must individualize the way they communicate by using the preferred channel and perception of each person. This is especially true in persuading employees to embrace a quality program. To achieve buy-in, leaders must individualize the way they communicate with every employee. These channels are also used in the various interaction or management styles discussed in the next chapter.

5

Interaction Styles

*"You don't lead by hitting people over the head—
that's assault, not leadership."*

Dwight D. Eisenhower

In his book *The Mastery of Management,* Dr. Taibi Kahler explains how each of the six types prefers to be managed and interact with others. He describes four classical management styles: the Autocratic, the Democratic, the Benevolent, and the Laissez Faire. The person using the *Autocratic* style gives commands and directives and encourages others to respond directly to her or him. This is a task-oriented style useful with those who require direction, structure, definition, or training. It has been the prevalent style in organizations since the beginning of the industrial revolution and frequently is used in crisis situations and with new hires and people who are just learning a new job.

The *Democratic* style is based on the principles of group participation and decision-making. The person using this style encourages interaction between and among others, solicits feedback, and fosters independent thinking. This participatory style encourages goal-oriented people to grow at their own pace. It also increases group cohesion and enhances morale by getting everyone to participate in setting common goals. Today, this style frequently is presented as the "right" style to use in an organization.

Individual feelings are more important than tasks to people who use the *Benevolent* style. These people assume that when people feel good, they do better work. They attempt to foster a sense of belonging in others by interacting in a nurturing and accepting way. This style works well with people who require unconditional acceptance. However, some people dislike mixing personal relationships with professional relationships and consider this style an invasion of privacy. In her book *On People Management,* Mary Kay Ash, the founder and chairman emeritus of Mary Kay Inc., describes how she used the Benevolent style almost exclusively in turning a $5,000 nest egg into a billion dollar company. Her principles of management were simple and revolutionary: "Care, consideration, and kindness build a highly motivated work force." Her guiding principle was: "Always say something personal when talking to someone, even if it is only to compliment her on her hair." Her golden rule in running the company was: "How would I feel if I were the employee?" Because many of her potential customers were Reactors, she hired Reactors as her sales people and used the interaction style that they responded to most readily. This was easy for her to do because the Benevolent style was the style she was most comfortable using. Hiring the right people and using the right interaction style in managing them allowed her to give absolute and total commitment to producing quality products and taking care of the bottom line.

The *Laissez Faire* style is the most non-directive of the four. People who use this style invite others to assume as much responsibility as they can handle. This style works well for self-styled, do-your-own-thing individuals and for people who resent authority and a lot of rules and regulations. This style invites independence and creativity; however, it does not provide the direction and structure that some people need. This style frequently is found in high-tech start-up companies. For example, the creation of the computer mouse came out of this style.

To date, no single interaction style has been identified to be effective with everyone. In order to be effective, leaders must use an individualistic interaction style to communicate. Workaholics and Persisters are most productive when their supervisors use a Democratic interaction or management style in which they participate in setting team goals and the paths chosen to achieve them. Reactors consider co-workers part of their extended family and are most productive in an environment in which everyone is nurtured as if they were members of one big happy family. Rebels are most productive when their manager uses a Laissez Faire management style in which they are encouraged to use their creativity in finding innovative solutions to problems with a minimum of direction and supervision. Dreamers respond well to an Autocratic Style in which they are told to do one thing at a time and are left alone to accomplish it. Promoters also respond well to an Autocratic style. Tell them the goal and the quick reward they will get for achieving it and then get out of the way. Interacting the same way with everyone is not the same as interacting with, or managing, them equally. Neither is it treating them fairly. (See Table 5.1.)

When team leaders and managers do not individualize the way they interact with their colleagues and employees and do not motivate each according to her or his needs, the employees may show signs of distress that are predictable and observable. Leaders who know the warning signs to look for and recognize the significance of behavior when they see it can quickly intervene to re-motivate the employee. We will explore ways to motivate each of the six personality types in Chapter 6.

Table 5.1 Interaction styles.

Type	Interaction Style
Reactor	Benevolent
Workaholic	Democratic
Persister	Democratic
Dreamer	Autocratic
Rebel	Laissez Faire
Promoter	Autocratic

©1982 Taibi Kahler Associates, Inc.

A political appointee leader in a department of the U.S. government decided the department needed a new mission statement. He told his staff to create one. They developed it without asking for input from department employees and, in the process, left out many key provisions of the old one. Ironically, parts of the statement they omitted were the main reason that several key career employees were working at the department. The leader, using an Autocratic style, announced the new mission statement but did not communicate it effectively. Many of the employees who heard of the new mission statement did not like it and refused to embrace it. Many key leaders in the department and many staff people did not hear about the new mission statement. When they heard about it via the grapevine, they were angry because they had not been consulted and because it did not show concern for people. They refused to accept it. Many of the career employees who were aware of it professed that they had a difficult time remembering what it was. By using an Autocratic style, the leader effectively alienated a large percentage of his employees.

The January 14, 2008 issue of the *Wall Street Journal* carried an article entitled "Why CEOs Need to Be Honest with Their Boards." The article quoted Dirk Hobgood, a governance and risk-management consultant and chief financial officer at consulting and executive search firm Accretive Solutions. He said, "In the past, CEOs had carte blanche to do what they needed to do to run the company. Today's CEO really has to work effectively as a team member with the board and keep them up-to-date and keep the players involved." In other words, the Autocratic style does not work with most boards any longer either. Board members want to be part of the decision-making process and want the CEO to use a Democratic interaction style. According to the article, they also want CEOs to be honest with them and not try to hide or downplay problems. Indeed, when James A. Kilts, the former CEO of Gillette Co. and Nabisco Inc., addresses groups of leaders, he gives the following advice. "Tell the truth."

Only Promoters and Dreamers, who make up 15 percent of the North American population, are comfortable with the Autocratic interaction style. The other 85 percent are not comfortable with it and some openly rebel against it. Workaholics need an opportunity to provide information and recommend and discuss possible options. Persisters need to express their opinions and want to be heard. Rebels hate to be told what they must do and Reactors often feel attacked when ordered around.

Only Workaholics and Persisters, 35 percent of the North American population, are completely comfortable with the Democratic style. Only Reactors, who make up 30 percent of the North American population, are comfortable with the Benevolent style, and only Rebels, who make up 20 percent of the North American population, are comfortable with the Laissez Faire style. Leaders who want to be effective with all of their staff members and all of their employees must use an individualistic style.

In an individualistic interaction, the leader matches the style he or she uses to the personality type of the employee. For example, with a Promoter the leader uses an Autocratic style. With a Workaholic or Persister, he or she uses a Democratic style. With a Reactor, the leader uses a Benevolent style. That is the style Mary Kay Ash used with her Reactor employees and it enabled her to turn her company into a highly successful behemoth. With a Rebel the leader uses a Laissez Faire style.

What would this look like? In Chapter 4, we talked about Sylvester Hopewell, the former president of the 100 Black Men of DeKalb County, Georgia. Sylvester used an Autocratic style with the Promoter members of his board of directors. However, many of the men who volunteered to be mentors for the students in the Leadership Academy were Reactors, Workaholics, and Persisters. With the Reactors, he used a Benevolent style and he used the Democratic style with the Workaholics and Persisters. Many of the boys in the Leadership Academy program were Rebels, Promoters, and Dreamers. With the Rebels he used a Laissez Faire style and with the Promoters and Dreamers he used an Autocratic style. This took a lot of energy on his part; however, everyone was happy and productive and the program is a great success. More than 200 young people who might have been lost to society have graduated from the program in the past 10 years or are in the program at the present time. Many of those who graduated have gone on to college or are gainfully employed in meaningful jobs. Many have returned to Atlanta and have volunteered to be mentors to the young people currently in the program. That is the ultimate test of the success of a program—that people who have graduated from it realize how effective it is and want to help those in the program who come after them. The program succeeded because Sylvester used an individualistic interaction style in dealing with everyone.

Flexibility in communication is the key to successful interaction. People who shift personality traits to meet the Personality Types of others invite open and successful communication. They also establish trust with their employees. In addition, people who use a wider range of their personality parts guarantee themselves less emotional distress. This requires a lot of energy on the part of the leader and leaders must decide for themselves whether the improved communication, quality, productivity, and profitability are worth that expenditure of energy. When they see the results, many effective leaders today believe it is.

According to the article cited above, CEOs who fail to change from an Autocratic interaction style to a Democratic interaction style increasingly risk being fired. According to a Booz Allen study quoted in the article, nearly 32 percent of CEOs who stepped down in 2006 worldwide did so as a result of conflicts with their boards. The forced departures were nearly always because of transparency issues. They represent a slow deterioration of trust resulting from the inability of CEOs to communicate effectively with board members. Typically there were multiple events where the boards felt left out or believed the CEO was leading them down a path. Failure to communicate with board members can also increase company liability. In a handful of recent lawsuits, judges have sharply rebuked CEOs who made big plans without informing their boards.

Nor is this just a problem with CEOs. At a vacation resort in Florida, the president of the board of directors treated the resort as his personal fiefdom. He stacked the board with relatives, made decisions without discussing them with the board or with the owners, and failed to communicate with anyone. The owners lost confidence in him and in an owner revolt replaced the entire board. Leaders must be able to communicate to be effective and they must individualize the way they interact with their staff, their board, and their stockholders.

This is especially true when leaders deal with the public. In her paper "Evaluation of the Public Review Process and Risk Communication at High Level Biocontainment Laboratories," Margaret Race discussed qualitative factors such as trust, familiarity, catastrophic potential, and individual control as having strong effects on perceptions and levels of concern about risks. As a result of her research, she concluded that "how information is shared may be as important as what is presented about a complex project" in getting projects approved. According to the researchers cited in her article, "Lack of communication and miscommunication with the public are major factors in failure, or near failure, of projects." She explained that citizen opponents of high-level biocontainment laboratories in Boston and Denver stated they were upset by the tone of their meetings and interactions with experts. They felt the experts were dismissive of their questions, considered their concerns baseless, and were telling them what would be done rather than discussing public concerns. They also expressed offense at being talked down to by "arrogant, condescending experts."

How can leaders use the concepts of Process Communication in dealing with the public? Race provides several suggestions. According to her research, the public's overwhelming concern is trust. How can administrators gain that trust? Race says her research shows that in those instances when the public was kept fully informed with accurate information, including accurate information about accidents that occurred at the laboratory, minimal resistance occurred. The resistance was greatest in those instances where administrators withheld information, tried to maintain secrecy about the project, and treated representatives of the public arrogantly and dismissively. "Repeatedly when information was withheld, dialogue began poorly and rarely improved without extensive work."

This is true in all interpersonal relationships: leaders with stakeholders, managers with employees, employees with managers, politicians with the public, family members with each other, teachers with students, and friends with friends. It is especially true for leaders. People do not want to be talked down to by "arrogant, condescending" people. When leaders use an Autocratic style, many people may feel that they are being attacked or that the leader is talking down to them. Leaders should use the Autocratic style only with Promoters and Dreamers and sparingly with everyone else.

This is especially true in establishing a Quality program in an organization. A Quality program cannot be imposed from above. Many people resent being told that they have to do something. They want an opportunity to express their views and be heard. This is particularly true in situations requiring significant change. Establishing a Quality program in an organization requires a significant change in the culture of the organization as well as in the processes. Even minor changes can be uncomfortable and stressful. To change the culture of an organization is especially stressful and frequently results in employees getting into distress. When that happens some employees will aggressively resist any changes; others will attempt to sabotage the changes so that they can say, "I told you it wouldn't work." Still others will try to disrupt the process of change by getting team members to distrust each other. Others will become confused and make mistakes, thereby reducing the quality of the products, and still others will shut down and not do anything until someone tells them what to do.

Leaders can greatly improve the likelihood that their employees will embrace change if they use an individualistic interaction style in proposing it. They can give the Reactors an opportunity to express their feelings and reassure them that they are part of the organization "family." They can provide complete information for the Workaholics and give them an opportunity to provide input. Quality, standards, and value are important to Persisters. With them, leaders can explain how a Quality program will improve all three of these and ask the Persisters for their opinions. Leaders can use a Laissez Faire style with the Rebels and make sure they have an opportunity to tell everyone what they like and do not like about the procedures that are being considered. Above all, leaders can make certain that they periodically inject some humor into the meetings. Finally, leaders can tell the Promoters how they will benefit personally from the change and give the Dreamers time to think about the changes contemplated and actively solicit their ideas. If leaders do this, employees will be much more willing to endorse the need for change and to support adopting a quality program.

In Chapter 6 we will explain how leaders can individualize the way they motivate each employee. By ensuring that every employee gets their needs met every day, leaders can increase the likelihood that their employees will support the leader's vision and will be willing to embrace a quality program.

6

Getting Buy-in

"I contend that all other things being equal we will work harder and more effectively for people we like. And we will like them in direct proportion to how they make us feel."

Irwin Federman,
former high-tech company CEO

As we have seen in previous chapters, each of the six personality types communicates differently, learns differently, and prefers a different management style. They also are motivated differently and do different things when in distress because their motivational needs are not met. If people are not motivated according to their individual needs, they will show predictable distress behaviors that can have a disastrous impact on the organization. At the same time, these behaviors are a good warning signal to the leader that the employees are being mismanaged. This provides an opportunity for leaders to change the way they interact with individuals to ensure that the staff members get their motivational needs met positively. It also enables the leader to take corrective action to stave off possible disasters in the organization. If leaders don't understand the significance of the behavior and take no corrective action, an employee can create serious problems for the company, including bankruptcy.

In one high-tech company in Virginia, senior staff meetings were confrontational. The vice presidents argued with each other and the meetings frequently descended into shouting matches that lasted well into the night. Dissatisfaction at the VP level was rampant and their spouses grew to hate the company. The CFO was a Reactor. Reactors want everyone to get along with each other and when people argue or fight in their presence, they may get into distress. As we will see in Chapter 9, Reactors in distress make mistakes. In this case, the CFO did not properly prioritize the way he paid the company's bills. He paid less critical bills first and neglected to pay the companies that provided the materials needed to make their products. As a result, the suppliers ultimately demanded payment for the materials before they would ship. Without raw materials, the company could not make their products and eventually went bankrupt. The CEO had a vision, but he did not understand the importance of ensuring that employees got their needs met. Nor did he recognize the distress symptoms or the possible consequences of his negative leadership.

MOTIVATING THE SIX PERSONALITY TYPES

Workaholics

Workaholics need to be recognized for their hard work, their good ideas, and their accomplishments. They need to hear, "Good job; well done; great idea." Time is important to them. They need to know when things are due and they expect meetings to start and end on time. They structure their day and they may become frustrated when their planned schedule is interrupted without warning or when others are late for meetings. A senior manager at one U.S. government department, a Workaholic, reached retirement age and people began asking him when he was going to retire. Instead of telling him what a good job he was doing, people were suggesting he should retire. He began working 14 hours a day, 7 days a week to show everyone how valuable he was. Eventually he had a heart attack. After he recovered from the heart attack and returned to work, his superiors suggested that he take a medical retirement. Again, instead of being told what a good job he was doing, he was being told that people did not want him. He began working 18-hour days, 7 days a week and his wife divorced him. He continued to work longer and longer hours until he had the heart attack that killed him.

Persisters

Persisters also need to be recognized for their accomplishments and their good ideas, but they also need to be recognized for their commitment, dedication, and values. They would rather be respected than liked. They respond well to "Great idea: I admire your commitment to your ideals" and "I respect the way you not only talk the talk, but also walk the walk." They cannot work for an organization that does not practice what it preaches or for leaders they do not respect.

The national sales manager of a $1 billion company on the west coast of the United States was being groomed to succeed to the vice-presidency of the company. In all the years he worked for the company, no one ever told him he was doing a good job. They gave him the maximum annual bonus, but no one ever sat down with him and discussed his job performance, his future, or his career ambitions. He was not getting his Recognition of Work need met and he left the company to take a lesser paying job with another company.

Reactors

Reactors need to know that people like them, not for anything they have done but simply because they are nice people. They need to hear from their significant others every day that they are loved. In the work place they respond well to, "I'm glad you are here. You really care about our employees/clients/patients." Leaders can help them meet their Recognition of Person need by spending time talking to them about whatever they want to talk about. Frequently this will be about family or other people who are important to them. Fifteen seconds a day of getting this need met is minimum dosage, but more is better. If Reactors have not had their Recognition of Person need met for a prolonged period of time, they may need significantly more time than that. A vice president of Hughes Network Systems in Maryland reported that some days he found he had to spend as much as an hour at the beginning of the day talking with his Reactor secretary about her family. He said he did not want to spend that much time with her, but he had learned that the time he spent listening to her and talking with her might be the most important time he spent all day because she was so much more productive.

Reactors also need sensory stimulation. They need to work and live in a cozy, nest-like environment. They like flowers and plants, soft soothing music, and comfortable chairs. One of the authors, Judy, taught chemistry in a classroom in the basement in a room with no windows. The other teachers called the classroom "the dungeon" and refused to teach in it. The Reactor students in the chemistry class were so uncomfortable in the classroom that they were not able to concentrate. Fortunately Judy, as the chair of the science department, was able to design a new science wing for the school. She insured there were windows in every classroom so that the Reactor students could look at the trees and sky outside. The grades of the Reactor students improved by at least a full grade each.

Dreamers

Dreamers are not motivated by any of these things. Their primary motivation is private time and private space. In a word, Dreamers need Solitude. Unfortunately, they frequently are assigned to desks in high-traffic areas in the workplace. To offset this, one of the authors, Joe, used to send his Dreamer secretary on errands periodically and tell her to take her time coming back. She walked through the halls and did not see any of the many people who passed her, thereby getting her Solitude need met daily. If Joe were going to be out of the office for a prolonged period of time, he might tell her to work in his office while he was gone. In these ways she got her Solitude need met every day and was much more productive as a result.

Rebels

Rebels are motivated by having fun and by being able to use their creative energy in positive ways. They are easily bored and need at least two hours a week of playful interaction with their peers. They are a leader's most creative employees, but frequently march to a different drummer than the other five types. If they do not get their needs met, Rebels may become uncooperative and refuse to do any work. A team leader at a U.S. government agency reported that a Rebel employee who had previously worked in several different branches was being transferred into her branch because none of the other managers wanted her working for them. The team leader allowed her to decorate her office with colorful posters, arranged for her to have a special assignment out of the office one day each month, encouraged her to think creatively about their projects, and communicated with her in the Emotive channel every day. The employee began volunteering to undertake routine tasks that no one else wanted to do and made several creative suggestions to resolve some of the technical problems the team was working on.

At one NASA Center, a Rebel employee used to keep several empty soft drink cans on her desk and every morning when she came to work she would arrange the cans creatively in the shape of various animals. One day she made them into a camel. Another day she arranged them as a horse. Her team leader did not mind, but one day the division chief walked past her office, saw the cans, and ordered her to get rid of them. She objected, but he insisted; for the next year she constantly complained about not being able to decorate her office the way she wanted. Moreover, her work was affected. She had been an important member of the team but suddenly became a disruptive influence and stopped making suggestions to help the team solve problems. The team leader knew he had to do something to motivate her to participate positively again. He told her he could not over-rule the division chief on the soft drink cans. Instead, he gave her a mechanical toy to put on her desk. The employee was delighted. She liked the toy and played with it whenever she needed a pickup during the day. Her negative behaviors stopped and she once again became a valuable member of the team.

A California film company that produces feature cartoon films has a large room filled with games that the employees use to "recharge their batteries" throughout the day. The company needs the creativity of their Rebel employees in order to produce successful high quality films. They have found that these employees are much more creative when they have an opportunity to play periodically during the day. Sometimes employees play the games for an hour at a time. When they return to work their creative juices are flowing.

Promoters

Promoters need action and excitement, a rush. No working 30 years for a gold watch for them. They respond to challenges and work for short-term goals with quick rewards. They need to see how they will benefit personally from whatever they are told to do. If they don't get their Incident need met in the workplace, they become disruptive and may not carry their weight in team projects. In fact, they may abandon their teammates and leave them to fend for themselves.

The vice president of sales and marketing for a Virginia accounting firm recounted the following story. One of his best sales people went to Baltimore to close a sale with a Baltimore company and the company signed a sizable contract. As the salesman was returning to Virginia, he heard on the radio that an accident on the Interstate had backed up traffic for seven miles, causing a three-hour traffic delay. The salesman realized that the office would be closed by the time he got there and that everyone would be gone. He went straight home instead, arriving at exactly 5:00 p.m., the normal office closing time. Just as he entered his home, the phone rang. It was a Promoter colleague calling to see whether he planned to return to the office. The salesman asked his colleague to tell the Vice President and the President that he had the signed contract and, because of the backup on the Interstate, he would bring it to the office in the morning. Instead, the Promoter told the President that the salesman had not gone to Baltimore and did not have the contract. Instead, he had spent the afternoon at home. When the salesman took the contract to the office in the morning, he expected to be complimented by the President and Vice President. Instead, a very angry President demanded to see him and accused him of shirking his responsibilities to the company. When he saw the signed contract and heard the story, the President said, "You have to watch that guy. You can't trust him."

What happened in the relationship between the Promoter and the President of the company that resulted in the Promoter acting this way? In an effort to motivate the Promoter salesman, the President had set a nearly impossible sales goal for him, challenged him to accomplish it, and promised him a $30,000 bonus if he achieved it. The bonus, when added to the Promoter's salary and the commissions he received on the extra sales, meant that he would have earned more that month than the President. The President, a Promoter himself, decided he would not pay one of his staff more than he paid himself. He denied having promised the bonus and refused to pay it. The Promoter salesperson then set out to destroy the sales team. He succeeded and eventually was fired.

Persisters can't work for people they do not respect. When the President did not honor the commitment he had made to the Promoter salesman, the Persister lost respect for him and left the company to become the sales manager of another firm. As a result, the President lost his two best sales people and most of the sales force because he did not honor his commitment.

Table 6.1 shows the motivational needs for each of the six personality types. Research shows that employees of all six types can do well on teams and in the workplace when leaders motivate according to their needs. A working knowledge of the concepts of Process Communication enables leaders to understand staff and team members so that they can address the motivational needs of each type every day. To do so, leaders can ask themselves the following questions:

1. How can I provide personal recognition for the Reactor?

2. How can I give recognition for work and provide time structure for the Workaholic?

3. How can I ensure that the task is meaningful for the Persister?

4. How can I provide reflection time, space, and structure for the Dreamer?

5. How can I ensure that the task is fun for the Rebel?

6. How can I incorporate action and excitement for the Promoter?

If leaders will do this, employee motivation and job performance will improve and employees will stop their negative behaviors. This will allow leaders to spend more time focusing on goals and less time putting out fires. Savage, in 1991, said, "Learners who get their needs met in school seldom cause trouble, because doing something that interferes with getting a need met is not in their self interest." Although Savage was talking about students in the classroom, his comments are equally applicable in the workplace. Dr. Jonathan Knaupp, a professor at Arizona State University, said, "We can give employees what they deserve or what they need. If we give them what they need, they will deserve more." This is the key to establishing relationships and to the success of every employee—helping them get their motivational needs met every day.

Table 6.1   Motivational needs.

Type	Needs
Reactor	Recognition of Person, Sensory
Workaholic	Recognition for Work, Time Structure
Persister	Recognition for Work, Conviction
Dreamer	Solitude, Clear Directions
Rebel	Playful Contact
Promoter	Incidence, Action

©1982 Taibi Kahler Associates, Inc.

In their book *First Break All the Rules,* Marcus Buckingham and Curt Coffman describe the results of extensive interviewing done by The Gallup Organization to determine the effectiveness of a workplace. They found that if employees could answer twelve questions positively, they worked for an effective manager in an effective organization.

All of these questions can be related to the needs or character strengths of the six personality types. For example, "At work do my opinions seem to count?" clearly refers to the Conviction need of the Persister. "In the last seven days have I received recognition or praise for doing good work?" refers to the Recognition of Work need of the Workaholic and Persister. "Do I have a best friend at work?" and "Does my supervisor or someone at work seem to care about me as a person?" refer to the Recognition of Person need of the Reactor. "At work do I have the opportunity to do what I do best every day?" refers to the strengths of each of the six types. For example, for the Rebel it might mean to be creative and have fun. For the Promoter it might mean lead, sell, or be involved in challenging or exciting projects. For the Reactor it might mean use excellent interpersonal skills or show concern for other people. For the Dreamer it might mean be reflective, conceptualize ideas, and work alone. For the Workaholic it might mean analyze data or work with numbers. For the Persister it might mean work on a project that is important or challenging, one that will have impact. Helping employees get their needs met greatly improves their job satisfaction, their desire to produce quality work, and their willingness to adjust to new ideas.

The vice president in an aerospace manufacturing company in California was very work oriented. One of his staff members was a Reactor who was more family oriented and who always wanted to talk about personal things. The vice president dreaded having conversations with her because they were long and drawn out and were all about personal information. The V.P. began to spend about five minutes with her at the beginning of each meeting, building rapport and talking about personal matters. One day she took the Reactor to lunch and talked about her hobbies, her family, her weekend, and other personal things. The Reactor's morale soared and she greatly improved her job performance.

Rose Wynne Brookes, the vice president of the finance company mentioned in Chapter 4, had a staff member who is a Workaholic with Promoter second in her personality structure. Rose Wynne sent her to attend various large company-wide meetings. The employee got the action she needed by attending the meeting and the excitement of having exposure to many others in the company. Whenever feasible, Rose Wynne allowed her to stay an extra day to socialize. In this way Rose Wynne helped her get her Promoter need for Incidence met. Another staff member was a Persister. Rose Wynne frequently praised her for the value she brings to meetings. Still another staff member was a Persister who has Rebel on her second floor and Reactor third in her personality structure. This employee had no concept of time and was always late for meetings. Rose Wynne ignored her tardiness because she was productive and creative and her work always was completed as needed. Rose Wynne learned that the employee's family was very important to her; she gave the employee and her daughter a spa treatment together. She also started going by her desk every Monday to hear about her weekend.

Major General Gale Pollock (retired), the former Acting Surgeon of the U.S. Army Medical Corps, learned of the concepts of Process Communication as a major, just before she was about to take over a dysfunctional department in an army hospital. Many of the nurses in the department were Reactors who were not getting their needs met. Major Pollock made sure that every member of her department got his or her needs met every day and successfully turned the department around. She did such a good job leading the department that the army reached two years below the promotion zone to promote her to Lt. Colonel.

General Pollock continued to use the concepts throughout her career and was promoted to Major General and named Commandant of the Army Nurse Corps. Subsequently she was named the Deputy Surgeon General of the Army, the first woman and the first nurse to hold that position. When the Surgeon General was forced to retire, she became the Acting Surgeon General. Because of a series of negative media reports about medical care in the Army and because of drastic budget cuts to military medical stations, morale in the Army medical corps was low. To counter this, every two months General Pollock sent a five-minute video to the medical staff informing them of developments and recounting all the good things the Army medical corps was doing in supporting the troops in Iraq and Afghanistan. She praised them for the good job they were doing; reminded them of how valuable they were to the military; told them how much she appreciated their commitment to, and performance of, their duties; and told them how much she appreciated their concern for the wounded troops and the family members left behind. Because everyone was getting their needs met, her messages were eagerly anticipated. Moreover, the messages had the desired effect on the staff of the medical corps. Morale soared and staff re-dedicated themselves to serving the troops and carrying out General Pollock's vision.

Ensuring that people are informed and get their needs met every day is the key to establishing trust and gaining followers to help leaders realize their vision for their organizations.

Because of a phenomenon Dr. Kahler calls *phase*, the current motivation of the leader in Figure 2.1 is that of a Promoter. As North Americans go through life, two thirds of them experience "a phase change." When this happens, they move to the next floor in their personality structure and essentially operate with a new driving force. While experiencing a phase change (phasing), people very often exhibit intense negative behaviors associated with their current personality type. After a person has completed a phase change, he or she will have new motivational needs and a new

Table 6.2 Motivation strategies by personality type.

Workaholic	Promoter
Good job	Bonus
Great idea	Make deals with
Well done	Exciting/challenging projects
I appreciate your hard work	Quick rewards
Start/end meetings on time	Short-term projects
Thank you for making the deadline	Break long projects into short segments
Great analysis	Challenging assignments
You are really great with numbers	You are the man
Great report	This is right up your alley
Thanks for keeping our accounts up to date	I have a challenge for you
I know I can count on you	Salesman of the month award
What are our options	
That's logical	**Reactor**
Great reasoning	Spend time talking with them
Good thinking	I appreciate you
	I appreciate your sensitivity with people
Persister	You have great people skills
Great job	You really care
I admire your dedication and commitment	You do so much for the morale here
You always do quality work	You are terrific
That was an outstanding report	You look very nice today
What is your opinion?	Those are beautiful earrings
What do you believe we should do	That is a gorgeous sweater
I admire the way you practice what you preach	That dress is very pretty
You talk the talk and walk the walk	That is a great necktie
I know I can count on you.	You always dress so stylishly
Great idea	That suit is very nice
Rebel	**Dreamer**
Let's have some fun	Take this to…Don't come back for 20 minutes
I love your creativity	Go back to your office and do (1 thing)
Great sketches	Prioritize tasks for them
You have the most creative ideas	First do this, then do this
That is so cool	Go to your office and shut the door
You rock	Hold all phone calls for 10 minutes
Have you heard the one about…	Go for a walk during lunch (alone)
Mechanical toys/games on desk	Go to a quiet place (library or reflection room)
iPod with earbuds to listen to music	
Fun posters in office	
Individuality in decorating office	
Fun assignments	

sequence of negative behaviors. This new phase lasts from two years to a lifetime.

Phasing also might be a contributing factor in many situations in life—divorce, burnout, and mid-life crisis to name a few. When people experience a phase change, they retain and strengthen the positive attributes and behaviors associated with past phases; many aspects of their personality remain the same. For example, their character strengths and their preferences for interacting with others are always with them. Their favorite way of communicating and the most well-developed parts of their personality also remain the same. So does their preferred learning style, their perception of the world, and their favorite working style (in groups, alone, or with one other person). The concept of phasing can explain how individuals can be the same person throughout their lives even though their dreams, aspirations, careers, and personal goals may change. When people experience a phase change, they experience changes in motivation and in the way in which they handle distress.

What triggers a phase change? According to Dr. Kahler's research, 98 percent of phase changes are the result of prolonged severe distress. The following story illustrates the impact of phase on the life of a leader in the military, the United States Government, and corporate America.

"I was born a Persister. As a Persister I learned very quickly that life was serious and I took everything seriously. I developed a sense of direction, mission, and conviction and was motivated by working hard and dedicating myself to causes I believed in. Values, beliefs, dedication, commitment, respect, and community service were important to me. I was active in my church and in boy scouts and I served on the student council in school. This dedication to causes has been a continuous theme throughout my life.

"When I was four years old, my father suffered a spinal injury that disabled him for the rest of his life. I quickly concluded that it was up to me to support the family. I took on any job I could find to earn money for the family and by the time I was six I was supporting the family. I weeded gardens, mowed lawns, shoveled snow, caddied at the local golf course, and ran three paper routes. When I was seven or eight years old I began to wake up nights, unable to sleep because I was afraid my family would starve because I could not earn enough money to support them. I began to criticize and attack others for their lack of commitment and dedication. Finally I dealt with my fear and moved to the next floor in my personality condominium, the Workaholic part of my personality structure. I had completed my phase change. I was still a Persister, but now I was operating in a Workaholic mode.

"In a Workaholic phase, I began to be more responsible, logical, and organized. I was still conscientious and dedicated and continued to work hard for something I believed in and I was still motivated by being recognized for my work. However, now time began to be important to me. Suddenly, I needed to be on time for everything. Being late was unthinkable to me. On dates, I would arrive around the corner from my date's house a half hour early to ensure that I was ringing the bell at her house at the exact time I said I would be there. My date was never ready, but that was okay because I was on time. I also began to excel in mathematics and in logical problem solving and I began college intending to major in physics.

"After several years in a Workaholic phase, I began to be depressed because things were not working out as I thought they should. I was working very hard as a carpenter building houses, in a factory making sporting gear, in a graveyard digging graves, on a construction crew paving roads and cleaning sewers, as a farmer raising chickens and selling vegetables, yet my father died and my mother was seriously ill. I became critical of others and began to attack them for not thinking clearly and not caring about their work. Finally, I dealt with my grief and I moved to the next floor in my condominium—my Promoter floor.

"I had always been a good athlete, but now I intensified my commitment to sports. I was still a team player, but now I wanted the challenge of guarding the other team's best player on defense and I wanted to be the one with the ball in my hand for the game winner at the buzzer. I began to participate in high-risk activities like drag racing, betting on horse races, and playing in high stakes poker games. To my surprise, I became more popular with my classmates, especially with the women in my class. I had no trouble getting dates and I enjoyed playing the field. Whenever I stopped dating a girl, I always left on good terms with her and maintained a cordial relationship, even after we broke up. Because of my newfound popularity I ran for president of the Men's Club and I won. The following year I ran for president of the senior class and I won again.

"The country was at war when I graduated from college. I believed in the mission and craved the excitement of fighting for a cause I believed in. After graduation, I went to officer candidate school and served five years in the Navy. My ability as a leader was recognized and I won commendations and was promoted several times. After my release from active duty, I served in a variety of exciting management and leadership positions in the government. However, I really wanted the challenge and excitement of laying everything on the line to run my own company. I relished the challenge of having final responsibility for my success or failure and the success or failure of the company. That's where I am today—president of a very successful company. Although I was successful in every position I held in my career, there were some employees I was not successful with. I never understood why I was missing them. Thanks to Dr. Kahler, I now understand how I missed them. More importantly, I understand what I could have done to reach them. I now use these concepts very successfully to reach all of my employees and everyone I deal with."

When people experience a phase change their motivation changes and the motivation of their phase becomes their driving force. Although everyone has all eight of the needs mentioned earlier in this chapter, some are more important than others. Which are most important to an individual? That depends on their personality structure and the phase they are in. Phase needs are most important, followed by their base needs. If they have experienced more than one phase change, then the needs associated with the phase they have staged through are next most important. These needs are followed in ascending order by the needs of the other parts of their personality.

In this example, the leader is a Persister who has staged through Workaholic and is in a Promoter phase. When he was in a Persister phase his most important need was the Persister needs of Conviction and Recognition of Work. In a Workaholic phase, his need for Time Structure and Recognition for Work was most important. In a Promoter phase, his current motivation is that of the Promoter. Therefore, his most important need is for Incidence—a lot of excitement in a short period of time, a "rush." His Persister Conviction and Recognition of Work needs are next most important, followed by his Workaholic Time Structure need. If the rest of his personality structure were Reactor, Rebel, and then Dreamer, the rest of this leader's needs, in descending order of importance would be, Recognition of Person and Sensory, Playful Contact, and Solitude.

How does a phase change impact business relationships? Two friends decided to start a business together. One was a Persister in a Persister phase. He had Workaholic second in his personality structure and Promoter third. He had Dreamer as the least well-developed part of his personality. The other was a Persister who was in a Workaholic phase. He had Dreamer third in his personality structure. They started their company and worked well together. Their company was prospering. Then the second partner experienced a tragedy. Two of his children were killed in an accident. He internalized his grief and continued to work with his partner, but he was spending almost all of his time criticizing everyone for not thinking clearly and for being stupid. The company began to suffer. The other partner began to attack him for his poor attitude and their friendship suffered. When his wife suffered a nervous breakdown he could no longer contain his grief and he began to cry uncontrollably. He then became a candidate for a phase change and he entered a Dreamer phase. His motivation changed and he lost interest in the business. His Persister partner no longer was able to communicate with him and began to argue with him. His partner began to attack him for his lack of commitment to the business and he finally sold his share of the business to his partner.

David Dingwall is the Rector of an Episcopal church in Maryland. In an effort to promote a more effective parish council, he had the council members attend a Process Communication seminar. This provided him with an understanding of the personality structure of each of the council members and allowed him to communicate with them more effectively and meet their needs in parish meetings. One member of the council, a Persister in a Persister phase, was in severe distress. He attended every parish gathering and gave his opinions of everything, whether he had anything to contribute or not. After a while people began to avoid parish functions when they knew he would be there. Rather than trying to discourage him from speaking, David began to ask his opinion, thereby helping him get his Persister Conviction need met. When one of his ideas was adopted, eventually becoming one of the most successful programs the parish offered, it gave the council member recognition for his ideas and additional status in the parish. Because his opinions were being sought and listened to, the council member stopped trying to force his ideas and became more willing to listen to the ideas of others. Now, his presence at church functions is valuable and welcome.

David also used Dr. Kahler's Personality Pattern Inventory in hiring a new administrative assistant. Knowing her personality structure enabled him to talk to her in her channel and perception and make certain he helped her get her motivational needs met every day. This has made his dealings with her much better than they would have been and has resulted in the assistant being much more productive than she would have been. David now intends to use the profile whenever he has a position open.

Brenda Dingwall, David's wife, was asked to plan, develop, and institute a summer camp for children of incarcerated parents. The camp had been in existence for one year and there had been significant problems with core team dynamics the first year. The core team consisted of a Persister in a Workaholic phase, a Rebel in a Persister phase, a Reactor in a Rebel phase, a Dreamer in a Dreamer phase, a Persister in a Rebel phase, and the former director of the camp, a Reactor in a Persister phase. Several of the team members were in considerable distress and the team was not functioning well. Brenda's task was to engage the Rebels while meeting the needs of the Persisters, Reactors, and Workaholics in order to overcome the dysfunction of the team and get the team members functioning smoothly.

Brenda realized it was critical to allow the Rebels to play at the beginning of the meeting, to help the Persisters know that their opinions would be heard, to make sure the Workaholics knew the team would get their work done, and to let the Reactors know that they were valued as people. She called the team together and explained how she planned to structure meetings to ensure that everyone's needs were met so that they could become a productive team. She also asked everyone to suspend judgment about whether her plan would work for one meeting, with the understanding that they could revisit the process after the minutes of the meeting were released.

The cook was a Rebel in a Persister phase, so Brenda asked him to prepare "cool" camp food to begin the meetings. He served things such as star cupcakes, camp mud, and cookies. The camp chaplain, a Reactor in a Persister phase, led the team in saying grace as a camp song. In this way, Brenda was able to satisfy her need to have everyone know all of the camp songs and the Rebels were able to have fun. The meeting agenda was a list that was not in chronological order. They began the meeting with whatever held the most energy for people and continued until all the items on the list were discussed. They continued this approach with the training and schedule development.

By the time the camp began, the team was well acquainted with this process and the members were well prepared to deal with the campers—most of whom were Rebels. The campers and visitors to the camp commented on how incredibly creative and well run the camp was. The team was thrilled at the success of the program and every camper signed up to return the following year.

This is the key to effective leadership—establishing relationships and ensuring that every employee gets his or her motivational needs met every day. It is also the key to getting staff members to buy in to establishing a quality program in an organization. As noted in Chapter 5, establishing a quality program may require a significant change in the culture of the organization as well as in the processes. Change is uncomfortable! It also is stressful. To change the culture of an organization is especially stressful and frequently results in employees getting into distress. We will explain in Chapter 9 what each of the six types does when in distress and will explain strategies that leaders can use to keep them out of distress. Briefly stated, if leaders will ensure that every employee gets his or her motivational needs met every day, the employees are more likely to stay out of distress and will be much more willing to endorse the need for change and to support a quality program.

7

Developing Your Team

*"Successful leaders find it satisfying to watch people
learn, grow and succeed under their leadership."*

Roger Fulton, "Common Sense Leadership"

Nearly all successful leaders say that they consider developing the strengths and leadership abilities of their staff members an essential part of their job as leader. Indeed, many of the books on leadership list employee training and leadership development as requirements of leadership. Many leaders have found the concepts of Process Communication to be very helpful in accelerating employee growth.

Dr. Nate Regier, the Managing Partner of Next Element Consulting in Newton, Kansas, works continuously at developing the strengths and leadership ability of his staff members. He himself is a Promoter in a Workaholic phase and his staff is composed of Rebels, Workaholics, Persisters, and Reactors. He starts every staff meeting with "diamond drops," allowing staff members to give each other kudos for key relationships enhanced, jobs well done, deals sealed, quality customer service, and any other significant accomplishments. This accomplishes four goals:

1. It develops openness, trust, and cooperation among the staff members.

2. It ensures that all staff members get a battery charge for their motivational needs in every meeting.

3. It helps team members develop their ability to motivate others.

4. It helps everyone fully integrate the concepts of Process Communication so that they automatically apply the concepts with each other and with clients.

In meetings, the team reviews the minutes of the previous meeting paying particular attention to the responsible parties for action steps. This develops a sense of responsibility in every staff member and in the team. Nate encourages his team members to dream big. He ensures that they all know his vision and goals and he solicits input from everyone about how to accomplish goals. No idea is ridiculed or rejected out of hand. This encourages all of his staff members to develop creativity in dealing with real life problems as they arise. Consequently, everyone is constantly focused on finding creative ways to improve team performance and anticipate changes they can make to stay ahead of future requirements. Many leaders, including Nate, believe that successful companies change to meet changing conditions and that companies that refuse to change wither and die. By encouraging his staff to anticipate developments and be prepared to change, he helps the staff members develop a needed leadership skill.

Because most communication today is done electronically, Nate has his team routinely test outgoing e-mail messages with each other before they are sent to recipients. This further develops team openness and cooperation. It keeps each member of the team up to date on what everyone else is doing and helps them learn to think through and analyze situations and improve their ability to communicate using the concepts of Process Communication. To further develop the skills of his staff members, Nate often refers to real e-mail exchanges during supervision and coaching sessions with his employees so as to illustrate the power of the concepts and to help them grow in their ability to apply the concepts when communicating electronically.

Nate has found the concepts of Process Communication to be an extraordinary tool for managing conflict and for looking objectively at the mechanics of conflict. Being able to see where communication breaks down, offering tips for getting things back on track, and recognizing personal responsibility for miscommunication are powerful outcomes of using the concepts. With the diverse personalities on his staff, it is inevitable that there will be occasional conflict. When conflict arises, Nate seldom mediates. Instead, he stays behind the scenes and coaches the parties on how to take responsibility for their role in the conflict. He shows them how they can use the concepts of Process Communication to improve communication and he facilitates learning by encouraging them to try a new way.

When a person is in distress, behavior may become counterproductive. In a safe environment, one in which all team members are proficient in applying the concepts of Process Communication and are committed to team growth, Nate practices non-threatening intervention. For example, he might say to a Rebel staff member in an upbeat tone of voice, "Wow, I notice that you're doing a lot of blaming today. I wonder if I can supply the playful contact you need to get back into a good space. When you're in distress, we don't get the benefit of your healthy humor and your creativity." This can be both a reality check and a genuine offer of caring and support.

Nate also demonstrates to his staff how the concepts of Process Communication can be used to develop accountability, transparency, and trust by keeping agendas overt and making a genuine effort to meet others at their level. Transparency and high expectations can be intimidating for newcomers, but eventually they become a strong source of job satisfaction, accountability, and loyalty. Nate welcomes constructive criticism and tries to respond non-defensively and responsibly whenever he is given feedback. In this way he creates a safe environment that encourages others to do the same. As a result, constructive feedback is welcome at all levels.

Another way he develops the strengths and leadership ability of his staff is by speaking frankly about the way he individualizes communication and motivates each of them. Occasionally a staff member will complain that he is not fair, that he does not treat everyone the same way. He uses these opportunities to teach the importance of using an individualistic style in dealing with each of them. A typical response might be, "No, it is not fair. It is more than fair. I am trying to individualize the way I communicate with and motivate each person to get the best out of everyone. If I dealt with everyone the same, I would get mediocre performance at best. The team can't afford mediocre performance." He then explains what each person needs so that his staff members can individualize the way they deal with each other.

He gives these examples. "For the Rebel, we may move supervision to the coffee shop on the spur of the moment. For the Workaholic, I might allow extra time to co-create a slide show presentation. For the Persister, I might send a written note to recognize a specific customer service accomplishment. And I might invite a Reactor to ride with me to a client meeting to help me get a better feel for the group." These individualized approaches are overt, they can be discussed and evaluated for their effectiveness, and they can be modified creatively as necessary. This environment encourages his staff to appreciate different motivators, ask for what they need, and focus on their best performance instead of on what others are doing or getting. It also models for them tools they can use in their dealings with others.

Nate believes that a common language is a powerful tool for building team unity and that all team members must learn it, live it, and maximize its potential by building a culture around it. He chose the concepts of Process Communication as that language. He also believes that building a culture of effective communication requires rules of engagement, norms for behavior, and clear paths on which people can advance and pursue excellence. He demonstrates this daily for his staff and enjoys great job satisfaction each time someone gains a new insight, discovers another layer to the concepts, or changes the course of events in a positive direction by applying the concepts. The team members understand his vision and have developed a passion to explore, learn, and grow in developing an application of the model to the best of their abilities. They now use the concepts in all aspects of their daily lives.

The model has given Nate and all of his team members an appreciation for diversity. It has challenged their assumptions about individuals, has allowed them to move from a discipline and control mentality to an empowerment and motivation mindset, and has enabled them to see the potential within each person. It has enabled them to resist the pull of pride and self-justification in favor of effectiveness and growth. Finally, it has allowed them to understand that power struggles and negative behaviors are cries for help. They are desperate attempts to meet basic human needs.

Other leaders have used the concepts of Process Communication to improve the skills and leadership ability of their employees. The president of a California manufacturing company that makes metal gaskets and piping believed that along with expanding and increasing in profitability, they were experiencing growing pains. He believed he had the right people in the right jobs, but he was concerned that they were not operating as a great team. He asked the team whether they felt they were operating as a great team and they all said no. He asked whether they would like to set that as a goal and they agreed that they would. They decided that in order to function as a great team, they must respect each other by respecting the different strengths each member brought to the team, respect the differences in people, and genuinely care for each other. In his opinion, all members on great teams make a commitment to know each other well and allow others on the team to know them by opening themselves up to give and receive feedback and constructive criticism. The executive team members all learned the concepts of Process Communication and grew in their understanding of each other and their ability to communicate and lead their direct reports. The group also grew significantly in their sense of responsibility and their ability to resolve conflict. Organization and team humor increased exponentially and the team members came to share a common vision. The president's job was to establish strategy and organization values, model openness, and show that he cared for all members of the team. The president also grew and developed dramatically. Because of the growth of all members, they are on the way to becoming a great team. They all agree that the concepts of Process Communication were the vehicle for their growth, the final piece that carried the intimacy that allowed them to know each other and be known.

Brenda Dingwall is a leader at NASA and the wife of the rector of an Episcopal Church in Maryland. She has volunteered in various children's programs for many years. For the past few years, she has run a summer camp for children who have one or more parents in jail. Brenda knows that statistics are grim. Some 70 percent of children with one parent in jail and 90 percent of children with two parents in jail will someday be incarcerated themselves. In an effort to help some of these children, her summer camp uses the concepts of Process Communication. Each year the number of children who attend the camp has doubled.

One day the arts and crafts director called her to complain that two of the campers, a Promoter and a Rebel, were threatening each other and pushing and shoving during arts class. Brenda talked to the Promoter first. Knowing that Promoters need to look good to their peers, she told him that he would look really good to the other campers if he helped the arts and crafts director, especially because the director was new. She had stepped in that day to substitute for the original director, who had been injured in a car crash. She also told the Promoter camper that the real action was in being a leader, and that she knew he had the ability to be a very good leader. The Promoter then rejoined the group and she spoke to the Rebel. Because the Rebel's need is to have fun, she talked to this Rebel about how much fun he was missing because of his behavior. She also showed him how much fun he could have by helping people, especially because sometimes "you get cool stuff." He also rejoined the class.

When class ended, the arts and crafts director asked, "What did you do to those kids while you were sitting at the picnic table in plain view of everyone? They were entirely different kids when they came back." Brenda told the director about the concepts of Process Communication and what she had said to the campers. She explained why she had said what she said to each of them and why individualizing communication and motivation is necessary in order to be effective. The new arts and crafts director is the diocesan youth director, someone who communicates with and motivates the youth of the diocese every day. She immediately saw how she could be more effective if she were able to apply the concepts with her staff and with the youth. She said, "I want to learn that." Brenda arranged for the director to enroll in a seminar to learn the concepts and how to apply them. The director grew in her ability to lead her staff members and to develop the strengths of the youth of the diocese.

Hedges Capers, Jr. is vice president of a customer relationship management company in Chicago. Previously, he worked as a consultant helping corporations improve their profitability by improving the leadership skills of their managers and executives. The president of one company in California was concerned that his employees were not working to accomplish his vision for the company. The president was aloof and his employees felt he did not care about them and did not listen to their concerns or suggestions. In addition, he always seemed pre-occupied in his own thoughts and did not listen to their questions. To them, he seemed to be concerned only about the bottom line. The president wanted to improve his communication skills and asked Hedges for help.

One day at a company meeting, the president opened up the floor to questions. When an employee asked a question, the president brushed it aside with a curt "I'm not interested in that." Pretending that his hand was a gun, Hedges pointed his finger at the employee and loudly made the sound of a gun firing. He then turned to the president on the dais and said, "Don't worry, Mr. President. He won't ask another question." The president immediately understood what he had done and apologized to the employee. He explained that he was preoccupied with the company budget and a couple of other things and asked the employee to repeat the question. The employee did and the president answered it to the satisfaction of every employee. The president continued to grow in his interpersonal and communication skills and the company continued to prosper. Real leaders can influence up in a hierarchy as well as down.

Wright Anderson is the former Assistant Superintendent of schools in Vance County, North Carolina. When he was a high school principal, his school had a serious dropout problem; many of the students had no interest in school and were leaving when they turned sixteen. Because they hadn't graduated from high school, many were not able to find jobs. They faced an uncertain future and the possibility of crime and jail. Wright decided he had to do something to reduce the dropout rate in his school and asked the assistant principal to give him the names of the 20 students who were most often in trouble. He looked at their records and realized that many of them were Rebels and Promoters. The school was not reaching them and he decided that if he were going to reach them, he had to do something unorthodox that would pique their interest.

Wright decided to form a special club and include them in it. He knew it had to be a unique club with an unusual name that would appeal to the students. While watching the students in action, he realized that one of them, a Promoter, had the potential to be an effective leader. When they spoke in the hall, Wright told the student he was going to form a select club in the school and asked him to be the leader. At first the student eyed him with suspicion, but Wright continued by telling him he was going to call it the "Fools" club. He, Wright, was going to be the "Top Fool" and he wanted the student to be the "King Fool." The student thought that was cool and he agreed. Wright began to work with him to develop the student's leadership skills. As a result, the student became a positive role model in the school and soon persuaded the other so-called "trouble makers" to join the club. This gave him and the other members of the Fool's Club status in the school. More importantly, it showed all of them that someone in the school cared about them. They became interested in doing their schoolwork, stayed in school, and graduated.

One day, Wright saw the King Fool in the hallway with a woman he had never seen before. He wanted to talk to him so he called out, saying, "Hey Fool, come here a minute." The woman indignantly shouted, "Who are you calling a fool?" The young man replied, "It's okay, Mom. I'm the King Fool." The mother did not know what this was all about, but she appreciated the change in the young man's attitude. She said to Wright, "I don't know what you're doing, but keep it up. You have completely changed his life." Wright had found a way to develop the young man's leadership skills and to develop the strengths of other potential dropouts.

Later in the year, a new student enrolled in the school. He had just finished a jail term for assault and was not about to follow any school rules. The first day in the school he refused to take off his dew rag. Wright saw him in the hall and explained the school policy of not allowing students to wear hats or dew rags in school. The student refused to take it off and challenged Wright to make him. Wright asked him if he knew the King Fool. The student replied that the King Fool was one of his boys. Wright told him the King Fool was one of his boys, too, and suggested he talk to him. Just then the King Fool walked by. He saw what was going on and told the new student to take off the dew rag, that Wright was one of the good guys, and that he wanted him to do what Wright asked him to do. The new student immediately took off the dew rag. The King Fool also invited the new student to join the Fools club. The new student's attitude toward school changed.

Subsequently, Wright became the assistant superintendent of schools and he persuaded the superintendent to train all of the senior members of the staff and the incoming teachers in the concepts of Process Communication so that they would be able to establish relationships with all of their students.

The concepts of Process Communication can be applied in every aspect of a person's professional or personal life. In the next chapter, we will demonstrate ways the concepts have been used in advocating for change, fund raising, and many other areas.

8

Getting Results

"Never talk about the effort you and your team put into a project. Talk about the results—they are what matter."

Jack Welch,
former CEO of General Electric Corporation

In previous chapters we explained several of the concepts of Process Communication and gave examples of how leaders have used them in communicating their vision, in motivating employees, in improving company profitability and the performance of every employee, and in developing the strengths and leadership ability of staff members. These concepts are universally applicable. They can be used in every situation that requires interaction between two or more individuals. In this chapter we will describe how leaders of organizations have used the concepts in customer relations, personnel selection, self-awareness, negotiation, fund-raising, and in influencing procedural and cultural change—including persuading staff members to implement quality programs.

CUSTOMER RELATIONS

A large regional travel agency in California was spending so much money on customer service in order to retain the loyalty of their clients that they were almost functioning as a not-for-profit company. Upscale clients included movie stars, studio people, and other larger-than-life people who expected good service. Everyone was working hard and they had a lot of clients, but they were not very profitable. The president of the company went through Process Communication training and decided they were not doing customer service right because the agents did not know how to invite communication. She began by training all of her agents in Process Communication so that they could communicate more effectively with their clients. They learned how to use the concepts in their personal lives as well as in their business lives. The agents got the message that the company cared about them as people and was investing in them. Morale soared and the agents asked that everyone in the company be trained in order to support them better. Consequently, everyone in the company felt better about themselves and turnover dropped dramatically. The president was very happy with the progress, but felt they were still hearing too many complaints from their clients. She decided to try matching the agents with clients based on their personality types. In addition, she assigned the more difficult clients to the agents who were most proficient in applying the concepts of Process Communication.

One of the services her agents performed was meeting clients at the airport, helping them through the lines, and coddling them. One day, two very famous actors were traveling together. One was a Rebel and the other a Workaholic. The agent meeting them was a Workaholic with very little Rebel in his personality structure. The agent continually used the Requestive channel and the perception of Thoughts in talking with both. For example, he asked for information about the flight and provided various bits of local information in a matter-of-fact manner. The Workaholic always responded, but the Rebel actor got bored and ignored him. Frequently the Rebel spread his arms like airplane wings and pretended to fly away. Eventually, the Rebel made a snide comment and rudely interrupted the conversation between the Workaholic and the agent. It was clear that the Rebel actor was not happy with the agent. The consultant, who had done the Process Communication training, spoke to the Rebel actor using the concepts of Process Communication. He spoke to him in the Emotive channel and helped him get his need for Playful Contact met. He also suggested to the agent that he wear a Hawaiian shirt and talk to the Rebel playfully when meeting him at the airport. From then on the agent wore a Hawaiian shirt, shared jokes, spoke to him in the Emotive channel and even sang songs with him. The Rebel actor changed his behavior and stopped complaining about the agent and the "lousy service" the company provided. Other agents did the same thing with their clients and they all grew in efficiency. This reduced client turnover and the company began to attract new clients at less cost. Because of their increased profitability, the board of directors was able to command a significant premium a few years later when they sold the company.

PERSONNEL SELECTION

Wes Johnston is the executive vice president and chief operating officer of the American subsidiary of a South African company located in Virginia. His responsibilities cover every aspect of the business in locations from Canada to Brazil. Wes uses the concepts of Process Communication in every aspect of his life—in leading the company, in communicating his vision for the company, in setting goals, in working with the members of the executive team, in developing the leadership abilities of his direct reports, in personnel selection to ensure he places the right people in each job, and in his relations with his wife and his children.

Wes has developed an ideal PCM profile for each major role that reports to him. This includes executive level roles for businesses as large as $500 million, technical engineering roles, and administrative assistant roles. Whenever he interviews someone for a particular position, he first decides what strengths the person must have in order to perform the duties of the position at a sustained high level. With those strengths in mind he interviews the various candidates. During the interviews he asks each candidate to self-rank the six sets of character strengths in their personality from one to six. In his experience, candidates have been very honest in evaluating their strengths. This self-evaluation gives him a good way to match the strengths of the various candidates against the requirements of the position and reduces the likelihood that he will hire someone based primarily on how that person performed the duties of a different job that may have required very different skills and abilities. In this way, he has been successful in selecting people to fill key positions and the company is very profitable.

Myrla Cole Haury is the President of the Board of Directors of the Harvey County Domestic Violence/Sexual Assault Task Force Incorporated in Harvey County, Kansas. In the process of succession planning for an executive director to replace the founder of the organization, the board decided it wanted to improve communication among employees, management, and the board. The responsibilities of the executive director had grown enormously. In addition to a Safe House that provides shelter to victims of domestic violence and their children, they also have numerous outreach programs throughout the community. The task force had a strong executive director in the past and the board wanted the new executive director to be equally strong. Myrla also wanted a strong board of directors. Because the organization had grown so much, the board would have to start functioning more as a governing body and less like an advisory body. In anticipation of the changing role of the board, Myrla and her vice president decided they needed Process Communication training.

The board of directors had one strong internal candidate and several strong external candidates for the executive director position. After interviewing them all and checking their references, they hired the internal candidate. She had served the organization as coordinator of victim services for five years and was instrumental in the recent successes of the program and in the efficient operation of the Safe House and the outreach programs. After they hired her, they asked her to take Dr. Kahler's Personality Pattern Inventory to determine her personality profile so that as a board they could meet her psychological needs and oversee her work more effectively.

The Process Communication training also allowed Myrla to better understand herself and how others perceived her. She is a Persister in a Reactor phase and has always known that she was not like other women in some respects. She learned in the training that female Persisters represent only 2.5 percent of the North American population. Knowing that, she now accepts and values aspects of the Persister part of her personality that she had felt were too forceful. The information also helped her appreciate her Persister base personality for the valuable contributions it enables her to make to the organization. In addition, this revelation made her a better leader for the domestic violence/sexual assault work they are doing. Her goal now is to learn how to assert her beliefs, values, and opinions into the program in a constructive manner without losing her compassion for others, while at the same time getting the job done in innovative, imaginative, and artful ways.

The training also provided Myrla with the tools she needed to identify levels of distress in herself and in others. She now realizes that during the early stages of the hiring process she had descended into severe distress. Because she was certain that no one on the board shared her commitment to the program or to the clients they serve, she had threatened to resign. Fortunately, one of the board members was skilled in applying the concepts of Process Communication. He helped her get her needs met positively. This enabled her to see that other members of the board were just as committed to the program as she was, although they demonstrated their commitment in different ways. She learned that others with less Persister in their personality structures share her values, beliefs, and opinions. This allowed her to recognize the strengths of everyone on the board and honor what they have to offer.

As a result of this awareness, Myrla welcomes diversity on the board. Previously she had sought external diversity, and now she seeks personality diversity as well. Soon they will replace several board members whose six-year terms will be up. Myrla will be looking to increase internal diversity as she seeks their replacements. In the meantime, she will ask the other board members and the executive director to take the Process Communication training to facilitate their growth and improve their communication and leadership skills.

FUND RAISING

Sylvester Hopewell, whom we mentioned in Chapter 4, is the past president of the 100 Black Men of DeKalb County, Georgia. He used the concepts in recruiting board members and mentors for their Leadership Academy program, in communicating with parents, in communicating with the students in the leadership program, and in raising funds to support the various programs of the Leadership Academy. In fund raising conversations, he was able to assess the personality structure of the person with whom he was talking and shift to that person's favorite channel and perception. He explained his vision in terms that appealed to them. For example, when talking with Reactors he stressed how the leadership academy program helped people. With Persisters, he talked about the quality of the program and appealed to their shared belief that the country and the community cannot afford to let 35 to 50 percent of the young people in the community fall through the cracks. In making a presentation to Workaholics, he provided statistics about the number of young people the program was helping and told them of successes. With Promoters, he got right to the bottom line. He talked about the cost and the return on investment and described the action involved. When talking with Rebels, he described the fun activities they were doing with the young people in the education part of the program. The sponsors bought into the program and he was very successful in securing funding and volunteers.

He also uses the concepts in applying for grants. Although he doesn't often meet with the people who review the proposals, he assumes they are mostly Workaholics and Persisters. Believing this, he tries to show how his program aligns with their vision and provides them with a lot of data in the grant proposal. Prior to applying for a grant, Sylvester researches the grant organization or foundation to determine their mission and their vision. He then words his proposal to match the vision as closely as he can. For example, one of the organizations that provided funds to the program for the past few years is the Georgia Department of Labor. Their vision is to help ensure that everyone in Georgia has a job. Because Sylvester's goal of helping young people finish high school prepared to work aligns with the mission of the Department of Labor, he provided them with statistical data showing the success of the program and they approved the grant.

Brenda Dingwall, the volunteer we mentioned in Chapter 7, also used the concepts in raising funds for the summer camp she runs for the children of incarcerated parents. In 2008, the diocese gave her five minutes on the second day of their annual conference to describe her program and ask for financial support. She used the concepts throughout her presentation and when she finished the audience gave her a standing ovation. More importantly, individuals in the audience gave her $10,000 to support the program. How had she done it? She showed slides of the various activities of the program, showed kids having fun, provided data about the likely future of the kids unless someone intervened, explained her vision, tied her vision to the vision of the diocese, and asked for their support. Many of the participants listed her five-minute presentation as the highlight of the conference. The program is entirely funded by donations; Brenda used the concepts in several other presentations and raised a total of $20,000 to run the camp program.

The authors also used the concepts in raising funds for their universities and for various non-profit organizations they are affiliated with. For example, Joe was chairman of the 50th reunion committee at his college. At the 45th reunion, he learned that the class gift fund had only $125.62 in it. In the 45 years since graduation, no one had made any effort to collect money for the class gift fund. Using the concepts of Process Communication, Joe wrote his classmates and asked their help in raising funds so that the class could make a significant gift to the college. He wrote a general letter to the class three times a year for four years. Because most of the alumni were Reactors, Persisters, or Workaholics, in every letter he told them what wonderful people they were (Recognition of Person need for the Reactors) and described the growth of the college in number of students, number of buildings, and number of degree programs (Perception of Thoughts for the Workaholics). He also informed them of faculty and student awards and achievements and told them about the president's commitment to excellence for the college and her vision for future growth (Conviction need for the Persisters).

The donations began to come in. Every time one of his classmates made a donation, Joe wrote a personalized letter of thanks for the donation. For those he remembered from college, he mentioned some experience they shared. For those he did not know, he looked in the yearbook and wrote about something the donor had done in college. In every personal letter he provided a battery charge for the donor's motivational needs. The contributions increased. In subsequent general letters, Joe gave classmates a progress report on the amount of money donated, told them how wonderful they were for giving back to the college, told them what the committee planned for the reunion, asked for suggestions for additional activities, and set a new fund-raising goal. What was the result? The class was able to donate $85,000 to the college—the second largest gift in the history of the college. More significantly, the money was donated by 114 retired schoolteachers.

When Michael Brown was the former Vice President of Kahler Communications in Little Rock, Arkansas, he worked with television station AETN in a fund-raising effort. He helped them tailor their fund-raising requests to match the language and motivational needs of the personality types who were most likely to watch each program. They first analyzed the audience for each broadcast and then used the channel and perception of that type in wording the appeal. Finally, they included things in each appeal that matched the motivational needs of that type. What was the result? They tripled the amount of money raised compared to previous fund-raising efforts.

NEGOTIATIONS

The concepts also have been used successfully in negotiations. In most instances, negotiators do not know the personality types of the people with whom they are negotiating before they begin the negotiations. However, if they listen to how each of the negotiators talks, what perceptions they use when they speak, and what channels they are most comfortable using, base personality type and perhaps phase become apparent. This enables the negotiator to communicate in the best channel and perception, thereby reducing miscommunication and improving the likelihood that everyone will understand exactly what is being said.

Richard S. Johnston is a negotiator. He frequently mediates between parties who seem to be at an impasse in arriving at solutions that were acceptable to both parties. In 1997 he conducted a research project for a master's thesis at Antioch College in Ohio, to see whether it was possible to determine a person's base personality type within the first few minutes of meeting. He found that it was possible to accurately determine the base personality of people with whom he was negotiating within the first few minutes of conversation. This enabled him to communicate successfully and frequently enabled him to arrive at win-win solutions to problems.

Dr. Dianne Bradley, a professor at the University of Maryland, also used the concepts in negotiating settlements to problems. Before she joined the faculty at the University of Maryland, she worked in the special education parent negotiation department at a school system in the Washington, D.C. area. Her job was to negotiate settlements with parents who were not happy with the placement and services their children were receiving in the school system. When she attended a Process Communication training seminar, Dianne began to identify the personality types of the families she had worked with and realized they were displaying the very behaviors that were being described. She began to understand that behaviors she had previously labeled as irrational were really parents in distress. In the training, she learned how to use the concepts to invite people out of distress and saw how she could enable everyone to negotiate from a rational place.

After several weeks of practice using the concepts, Dianne often was able to identify a person's personality type over the phone judging by vocabulary and tone of voice. By the time mediation was set up, she had a good idea of the personality type of the parent. With this knowledge, she was able to open up the meeting using the appropriate channel and perception and give parents a "battery charge" for their psychological needs. For example, if she suspected the parent was a Reactor, she might offer a compliment or recognize how well a child with disability was cared for. If the parent was a Rebel, she started the meeting off on a light note in an upbeat tone. When parents started out critical of the school system or the school, she assumed they might be Persisters and complimented them on their commitment to obtaining the best education possible for their sons and daughters. She was never insincere; she believed that parents came to her office with the best interests of their children in mind, which also was the priority for the school system.

What were the results? Almost immediately she found that parents no longer in distress were willing to negotiate and compromise and she was able to conclude most mediation with a win-win agreement that eliminated the need for a due-process hearing. She was so successful with her negotiations that the people in her office began calling her the "mediation queen." She had a 99 percent success rate in reaching win-win agreements. By inviting the parents out of distress at the beginning of the meeting, instead of antagonizing them by saying things that would cause further distress, she was able to help everyone focus on the various options the school system had to offer and reach agreement on what was best for the child. (The distress behaviors and the intervention strategies are explained in detail in Chapter 9.)

In Apache Junction, Arizona, Dr. William Wright, the former superintendent of schools, decided to train everyone in the concepts of Process Communication: the teachers, coaches, and administrators and the classified supervisors of the secretarial, maintenance, custodial, and transportation departments. The administrators then evaluated the teachers every year on how well they implemented the concepts in their classes. After three years, annual employee turnover in the district was reduced from 43 percent to less than 5 percent, employee satisfaction and staff morale soared to an all-time high level, the failure rate in the seventh and eighth grades was reduced from 20 percent to less than 2 percent. Disciplinary referrals were significantly reduced so that fewer than two percent of students were in trouble on any given day. There was a 15 percent increase in student participation in athletics, graduation rates increased significantly, and students entering into post-secondary training increased from less than 19 percent to more than 43 percent.

As a result of these successes, the school system began using the concepts in negotiations with staff to settle salary and benefits questions. According to Dr. Neil Barwick, the former assistant superintendent of schools, the longest it took to negotiate salaries and benefits was seven hours after they began using the concepts in their negotiation process. In one year the district had a salary freeze for all employees and strict budget restrictions because of a downturn in the economic situation in the district. That salary freeze issue was settled in about six hours. The school system also created a Professional Advisory Council consisting of teachers and administrators; they met monthly to keep the lines of communication open and solve problems before they affected school operations. Everyone on the council was trained in the concepts of Process Communication and used the concepts to ensure that all participants were free of distress when discussing all issues. As a result, the council functioned very successfully.

The Persister manager of a Tennessee manufacturing company was not communicating effectively with the leader of the local union, a Rebel. The union leader perceived the plant manager as pompous and not interested in the employees. He called a wildcat strike nearly every day for about a year to protest various problems in the plant. The company had the plant manager trained in the concepts of Process Communication. The trainer suggested that the plant manager wear a Mickey Mouse watch as he walked around the plant, compliment the workers on the jobs they were doing, and ask about their families. Employees reported this change in behavior to the union leader and told him about the watch. The next time the union leader went to the manager's office to complain about an issue, he couldn't take his eyes off the watch. The plant manager noticed the union man looking at the watch and gave it to him. When the union leader tried to refuse, the plant manager pulled another one out of his desk drawer. They both wore their watches every day and there were no wildcat strikes at the plant for several years, throughout the duration of the union contract.

As these examples illustrate, the key to inviting people out of distress is helping them get their needs met positively. What each of the types does in three different levels of distress is described in the next chapter. We also explain strategies leaders can use to invite the six personality types out of each distress level. This frequently can be accomplished with a single sentence.

ADVOCATING CHANGE

The authors have a daughter who has Down syndrome. She was placed in a special education class in a regular school. The authors wanted her fully included in regular classes in their home high school, but the school system and the school board were opposed to doing this. The authors believed that they had to educate the board and the school system on the benefits of this placement. They began by assuming that most members of the school board were Persisters and Workaholics and thought that some of them might be in a Reactor phase. They offered public testimony to the board every two months and met with senior school system officials periodically to give them information about the benefits of inclusive education. They included something in every presentation to help all six types get their needs met positively. They also had their daughter speak to the board at the beginning and the end of each school year so that board members could see the improvement.

What were the results? At the beginning of the year the school board was eight to one opposed to having their daughter included in regular classes. At the end of the first year, eight members of the board were in favor of it and no one was opposed. One board member abstained for personal reasons. He privately explained his reasons to the authors and subsequently asked them to serve on his re-election committee. They agreed and he was re-elected.

The authors used this strategy in meetings with school system officials with similar results. In fact, after the first year, one administrator thanked the authors for showing the school administration what was possible. The school system wanted what is best for all students. When they saw that the student had a 25-point increase in IQ between the end of the eighth grade and the end of the ninth grade, and that she learned to read what everyone else was reading and to write short stories and term papers, they were impressed by the results and were willing to consider changing their policies.

Gladys Anderson was the principal of an elementary school in Wilmington, North Carolina. Gladys is a Reactor in a Persister phase. Because she cares about the feelings of her staff, she prefers to make changes incrementally rather than upset everyone by making a lot of changes at one time. Because her predecessor was a Workaholic with different strengths and a different management style, Gladys decided to share the structure of her personality condominium with the members of her staff and explain that the way she interacted with them would be different from the way her predecessor had. She felt that once they understood her structure they would understand why she managed differently and would accept the change that was going to make in their lives. She believed that once they understood how she perceived the world, they would understand the reasons for the changes she intended to make. In planning how to institute those changes, she took into consideration the difference in her management style from that of her predecessor.

Because Gladys is a Reactor who did not have understanding the mechanics of routine maintenance and support functions as a personal priority, she felt she had to make certain that others knew how to handle the mechanics of providing administrative support to the staff as well as she did so that the staff would not be bothered by little inconveniences. She also ensured that the Workaholics on her staff knew that she understood the ins and outs of administrative support and maintenance as well as her predecessor had, even though that was not her personal priority. Because she considered everyone on her staff and because she ensured that everyone got their needs met every day, she successfully made sweeping changes in the culture of the school. Morale in the school soared and the students improved their academic performance and significantly reduced their negative behaviors.

This is the way to persuade people to implement policy and culture change within organizations. This includes persuading them to implement a Total Quality program. Leaders who want to implement a quality program will be much more successful if they ensure that all employees get their needs met every day, if the information about the quality program is presented in the perceptions of each of the employees, and if the employees are invited to participate in the process of implementing the program. As we saw in Chapter 5, change cannot be mandated using an autocratic management style.

9

Followers in Distress

"When angry count to ten before you speak. If very angry, an hundred."

Thomas Jefferson

Thus far we have been talking mostly about the positive behaviors of the various personality types. However, when they get into distress, each of the six types has negative behaviors that are predictable and observable. Leaders who can identify the symptoms that indicate their followers are starting to get into distress can quickly intervene and head off further distress behavior before those individuals disrupt the smooth functioning of their teams. When leaders see the behaviors that we will describe in this chapter, they must remember that the people displaying the behaviors are still okay. The behaviors are a cry for help and a warning sign that people are being mismanaged, are having trouble dealing with something in another part of their lives, or are not getting their needs met positively. In many instances, this is what has triggered the negative distress behaviors. Understanding this, leaders can heed Jefferson's advice and not respond to the distress behavior by getting into distress themselves.

In his research, Dr. Kahler identified three levels of distress. Each has behaviors that are observable and predictable. According to Dr. Kahler, each of the six personality types experiences stress in a different way, leading to responses at each level of distress that are unique to that personality type. His research shows that these levels are sequential; people move through the first level of distress before moving to the second level and move through the first and second levels before moving into the most severe (third) level. In keeping with the condominium comparison described in Chapter 2, Dr. Kahler explains that beneath a personality condominium is a doorway (first degree) that leads to a basement (second degree) and ultimately into the cellar of distress (third degree).

Everyone, including leaders and their employees, experiences first-degree distress (the lowest level) many times during the day. Usually the distress lasts only a second or two and people return to the positive parts of their personality. Sometimes individuals experience the distress more severely and descend into the basement. Awareness of the signals that each type exhibits in first-degree distress can help leaders intervene before major problems ensue.

Second-degree distress is more noticeable and can be disruptive to team unity and productivity. Some employees attack others around issues of fairness and not being able to think clearly. Others push their ideas and attack people for not being committed to the goals of the team. When people attack others, they invite others to join them in distress. When that happens, some people make mistakes doing things they usually do very well. Others shut down. Still others do something to further antagonize other members of the team and others manipulate, con, lie, and stir up trouble with teammates. When leaders know the interventions to use to invite each of the six types out of first-degree and second-degree distress, they can eliminate friction on the team and improve team cohesiveness and the productivity and profitability of the organization. This is especially important when leaders are trying to implement a quality program in their organization. By understanding the behaviors described in this chapter, leaders will know when they are not communicating their vision effectively.

When employees of all six types get into third-degree distress, they feel depressed and useless. They may appear to be only going through the motions of their jobs. When this happens, they are not capable of thinking clearly and they may believe that others don't care about anything except themselves. At this point, they frequently stop caring about anything—their jobs, their appearance, or any activities. This usually happens when they have not gotten their needs met for a prolonged period of time and probably will require intense intervention to get them out of distress.

What are the warning signs that staff members are getting into distress? And what are the various interventions a leader can use to invite them out of distress, allowing them to be productive again? The rest of this chapter will answer those questions.

WORKAHOLICS

In first-degree distress, Workaholics expect themselves to be perfect and tend to put off doing things for pleasure until after they finish the job they are working on. They put off personal pleasure so much that eventually they begin to get into distress about it. They epitomize the old saying, "All work and no play makes Jack a dull boy." All work and no play frequently results in Workaholics getting into distress. When this happens, Workaholics do not delegate responsibility for job performance. They may appear to delegate, but really do not. For example, when telling someone to write a report they may add, "I want to see it before you send it." When the writer of the report shows it to her or him, the Workaholic in first-degree distress may completely rewrite it. Workaholics who do this think they are helping the writer learn to write more effectively. In reality, they are showing lack of trust and inviting the writer into distress. This may seriously affect the writer's morale and job satisfaction.

At one point in his career, one of the authors, Joe, worked for a deputy division chief who almost always was in first-degree or second-degree distress. He wanted to see everything before it was sent out and frequently rewrote things. He also talked in complicated sentences and people didn't understand what he was saying. In one staff meeting, the division chief interrupted him in the middle of a convoluted sentence and said, "For God's sake, speak English." From then on, the deputy was afraid to open his mouth in staff meetings. More importantly, he went into second-degree distress and after the meeting began to attack others.

Instead of attacking the deputy in front of the entire staff, what might the division chief do to invite him out of first-degree distress, thereby heading off descent into second-degree distress? To invite people out of first-degree distress, leaders can use the appropriate channel and perception to communicate with them. As we saw in Chapter 4, Workaholics' favorite channel is the Requestive channel. Their preferred perception is Thoughts. Knowing this, the division chief might ask something such as, "What does the data show?" Often this simple intervention of channel and perception will result in people coming out of first-degree distress.

In second-degree distress, Workaholics over-control; they put on a mask and attack people for not being able to think clearly, for a lack of neatness, for making mistakes, for being late for meetings or missing deadlines, or for not being logical or organized. In one large New Jersey insurance company an employee forgot about a staff meeting. His branch manager called to ask him why he wasn't there. As the employee rushed into the meeting, the branch manager attacked him for being late. The attack continued for about 15 minutes. After the meeting, the branch manager wrote a memo to the CEO, copying the employee's immediate supervisor and everyone in the chain of command. He complained about the employee's lack of respect and commitment, disregard for other people's time, and more. Did the CEO ask what was wrong with the employee or did he ask what was wrong with the branch manager? When people are in distress, they are not capable of thinking clearly. When a leader wants to talk with people who are in distress, he or she must first invite them out of distress or the employees will not accurately hear what is being said.

How can leaders invite someone out of second-degree distress? When people are in second-degree distress, they are advertising that they are being mismanaged or are not getting their needs met positively. Leaders should attempt to give them a battery charge for the need that corresponds to the behavior they are seeing. As we saw in Chapter 6, the Workaholic's needs are Recognition of Work and Time Structure. A leader can compliment them on something they have done well—a paper they wrote, a suggestion they made, a problem they handled well, a sale they made, and so on. When leaders help people in second-degree distress get their needs met, they usually will come out of distress immediately. However, leaders must remember that they cannot make people come out of distress, they can only invite them out. The employee makes the decision whether or not to accept the invitation.

One of the authors, Joe, has only been late for meetings twice in his entire life. Both times he thought he had a good reason for being late and was sure his bosses would understand. He was wrong both times. Once, an employee came to his office with a problem just as Joe was about to go to a staff meeting. Because it was clear that the problem could escalate if not resolved immediately, Joe helped the employee resolve the problem before going to the staff meeting. He entered the staff meeting three minutes late. His boss told him that if he could not get to meetings on time, he should not come at all and kicked him out of the conference room. After the meeting, Joe explained to his boss the reason he was late. The boss apologized and explained that his wife had just told him she was leaving him and planned to get a divorce. The lesson is that we seldom know what is going on in another person's life. Leaders cannot allow themselves to respond to another person's distress by getting into distress themselves.

PERSISTERS

In first-degree distress, Persisters focus on what people have done wrong and ignore what they have done right. They expect everyone to be perfect and believe that they need only help people correct what they aren't doing right and they will be perfect. After all, they already know how to do the things they are doing right; there is no need to talk about those things. When Persisters act this way, they think they are helping. In reality, they may be undermining their effectiveness. Because many Persisters rise to positions of authority, they can destroy the morale of an organization faster than the other types when they allow themselves to get into distress.

A leader who sees people focusing on what others are doing wrong and ignoring what they have done well can intervene by using the Persister's favorite channel and perception. As we saw in Chapter 4, the Persister's favorite channel is the Requestive channel; their favorite perception is Opinions. Leaders can ask, "What is your opinion?" or "What do you believe we should do?" This usually will result in the Persister stopping first-degree distress behavior and accessing the positive parts of their personality.

If leaders do not intervene and the Persister goes into second-degree distress, what will they do? In second-degree distress, Persisters put on an attacker mask and push their beliefs. When in second-degree distress, they frequently attack people for a lack of commitment to team goals, quality, values, or morals. For example, leaders might hear a Persister in second-degree distress say something such as, "Don't you care what's happening to our country?" or "Trust you? Not on your life. You've got the morals of an alley-cat." These are warning signs that the Persister is not getting her or his needs met. When they hear things like this, leaders can give Persisters a "battery charge" for their Conviction need or for their need for Recognition for Work. What might they say? "Ms. Persister, I admire your commitment to the ideals of this organization and I want to thank you for your dedication. I know I can count on you." Many times the Persister will accept this invitation and come out of distress.

The authors were running a Process Communication seminar for the staff members of an office in a U.S. government agency. One of the participants had a reputation for attacking others in the office and no one wanted to work with him. They avoided even talking to him whenever possible. His continual attack behavior was having a negative affect on team morale and was interfering with team productivity. Just before lunch on the second day of the seminar, the employee began to attack the trainers for something they said. The authors invited the employee to go to lunch with them and throughout the lunch gave him "battery charges" for his Conviction need and his Recognition for Work need. What did they say? They acknowledged that he was an experienced employee and an expert in several areas. They complimented him on his expertise and his years of experience and asked him his opinion on every subject discussed. He came out of distress and did not attack anyone for the rest of the seminar. For this strategy to be effective, the compliments must be sincere and as specific as possible. Generalizations are not nearly so effective as specific compliments.

In Chapter 8, Myrla Cole Haury, a Persister, described what she was doing when in second-degree distress. Briefly stated, she believed that no one on her Board of Directors shared her commitment to the program or to the clients they serve. She began to attack other board members for their lack of commitment, went into third-degree distress, and decided to resign. Fortunately, at least one of the board members understood what was happening, knew the concepts of Process Communication, and gave her a "battery charge" for her Conviction and Recognition of Work needs. When she came out of distress, they were able to show her that they were as committed as she was and she was able to hear their message and see their contributions to the goals of the organization and their commitment to their clients. She reconsidered resigning and instead put all of her energy into helping the organization carry out their mission of serving clients.

REACTORS

In first-degree distress, Reactors try to please everyone and have a hard time making decisions or asking for things directly. If two people come to Reactors with opposing recommendations, Reactors in first-degree distress may have a hard time deciding what to do. Reactors want everyone to like them and they frequently put the welfare of others ahead of their own. Instead of asking directly for a day off, Reactors say things such as, "Maybe I could have some time off sometime soon?" How can leaders intervene to invite them out of distress before they get into second-degree? As we saw in Chapter 4, the Reactor's favorite channel is the Nurturative channel and their perception is Emotions. Leaders may invite them out of distress by saying things such as, "How do you feel about this new policy?" or "Will you share your feelings with us about this program?"

In second-degree distress, Reactors make mistakes on things they know very well how to do. They may laugh at themselves inappropriately, call themselves stupid, or invite people to criticize them. The Reactor's needs are Recognition of Person and Sensory. Leaders can invite them out of second-degree distress by giving them a "battery charge" by saying things such as, "I'm glad you're here, you care" or "I appreciate your concern for the people in our organization." The authors frequently are able to invite Reactor women out of second-degree distress by complimenting them on their appearance, their earrings or necklace, or on some article of clothing they are wearing. Leaders also can invite Reactors out of distress by spending time talking with them about anything they want to talk about. Usually this will be about people they love.

Marti Szczur was a manager at the NASA Goddard Space Flight Center in Maryland. Most of her staff members were Workaholics and Persisters, and she communicated with them very effectively. However, she was having a difficult time communicating with one of her administrative assistants, a Reactor. She complimented her assistant on the good job she was doing, but that seemed to have no effect. On the contrary, the assistant made more and more mistakes. One example: Marti was scheduled to make a cross-country trip during which she would make sequential briefings at a number of the agency centers across the United States. She asked the assistant to confirm her travel arrangements and wrote out the dates she was to be at each site. Because the assistant made mistakes in everything she did, Marti knew she had to double-check the schedule to be sure it was correct. When she did, she found that the assistant had switched the dates for two of the stops.

Marti then attended a Process Communication seminar and learned that her assistant was a Reactor in second-degree and third-degree distress. She decided to change the way she talked with and motivated her. Marti had always planned her day on the drive to work and rushed past her assistant with a brief "Hello; how are you today?" After learning about Process Communication, she decided to change her behavior.

Instead of rushing past her assistant, Marti spent a few minutes each Monday morning talking with her about her weekend, observed when she had a new haircut or new shoes, and asked about her daughter. She also changed how she acknowledged her assistant's contributions when she did a good job. She thanked her, not her product. For example, she told her how much she appreciated her taking care of everyone in the office or how nice she was when greeting visitors and "making sure they felt comfortable." Occasionally, Marti brought in flowers as a thank you and she gave her a small budget to brighten up the office with plants, candles, and a candy bowl for visitors.

Within weeks, her assistant's attitude changed significantly. She was noticeably happier. Her work improved. Her appearance changed for the better and she became such an excellent assistant that a few years later she was promoted into an executive assistant position.

DREAMERS

In first-degree distress, Dreamers have difficulty figuring out what to do. When they are given more than one or two assignments, they become overwhelmed and may not know what to do first. They sometimes begin to do all of the tasks but don't finish any of them. This trait carries over to their speech. For example, they may start talking about one subject and then shift to an entirely different topic, frequently without finishing the sentence of the first subject. What does this sound like? "Lights are bright… Traffic was heavy… My wife said that … Yesterday my son went …"

Listening to Dreamers in first-degree distress can be painful for the other five types. Workaholics want information in a logical sequence and may think they are wasting time. Persisters want information that is important and may quickly lose patience. Reactors may feel sorry for Dreamers and want to console them. Rebels won't be having any fun listening and probably will tune the speaker out. Promoters want to get to the bottom line and may walk away. This is one reason Dreamers frequently are not called on to contribute to discussions. Because they do not volunteer their ideas unless invited to give them, their insights frequently are lost to the team.

What can leaders do to invite Dreamers out of first-degree distress? Again, the answer is to use their favorite channel and perception. The channel to use with a Dreamer is the Directive channel and the perception is Inaction. Leaders can say something such as, "Tell me one thing you did coming to work today." Obviously, leaders must tailor what they say to the subject the Dreamer is talking about. For example, if they are talking about a project, a leader might say, "Tell me one thing you did on the project." or "Tell me one thing you are going to do today to advance the project."

What do Dreamers do in second-degree distress? They shut down and sit there until someone tells them to do something. A senior staff officer in the U.S. Army Surgeon General's office, a Persister with the Dreamer part of his personality structure the least well-developed, had a Dreamer secretary who was not getting any work done. She started many projects, but did not finish any of them. She frequently sat there staring into space, seemingly immobilized. He began using the Directive channel and the perception of Inaction with her; he prioritized the list of tasks for her; and he helped her get her solitude need met every day. To his surprise and delight, she suddenly became one of his most productive employees. His secretary became happier in her job and in her work environment and was healthier as well as more productive. So was the staff officer.

Leaders may feel that it should not be necessary to prioritize tasks for their staff members. Joe certainly felt that way. However, he learned that the best way for everyone to be productive is to accept people as they are; play to peoples' strengths; and do whatever is necessary to overcome their shortcomings. For example, one director of a Boys and Girls Club in Maryland was about to fire one of his staff members because he never got his reports in on time. The staff member was very good in dealing with the kids in the club, his primary duty, but did not like to write. At our suggestion, the director assigned an administrative assistant to help write the monthly reports. The staff member was happy and introduced several new activities. The kids were happy and told their friends about all the fun they were having at the club. They brought friends into the club with them. Membership increased significantly and the club director was recognized for the increase in membership.

REBELS

In first-degree distress, Rebels may fidget, drum their fingers, become impatient, disrupt meetings in some way to attract attention, socialize with others off-topic, or not give people enough information to do the task they have been assigned. They may say things in a whiny voice. "This is hard" or "I don't get it" or "I can't." As managers, they may not give their employees enough information to do the job they have assigned them.

How can leaders invite Rebels out of first-degree distress? The Rebel's favorite channel is the Emotive channel and their perception is Reactions, that is, likes and dislikes. Leaders can say things such as, "Hey, I like it when you let me know that I'm going too fast for you to stay with me." Or "I like roller coasters, but not airplanes imitating them." In most instances, Rebels will accept this invitation and come out of first-degree distress. It's also important for leaders to know what Rebels don't like. Once Rebels tell their bosses what they don't like, they forget about it. Until then, it may fester like an open sore and may result in their going into second-degree distress.

What do Rebels do in second-degree distress? They blame, become stubborn, insist on their own way, disrupt meetings, and sabotage projects with an "I'll show you" attitude in order to get revenge. How can leaders invite Rebels out of second-degree distress? Help them get their need for playful contact met by sharing a joke, speaking to them in an upbeat and energetic way, providing opportunities for their creativity, allowing time during the day for some fun playing video games, allowing them to have games or fun things in their office, and allowing them to move around throughout the day.

A young woman in the training division of a U.S. government agency was uncooperative and disruptive, and was being shuffled from branch to branch because none of her managers knew how to communicate with her. Finally, she was transferred to a branch manager who understood the concepts of Process Communication. Before the employee arrived, the manager put some bright posters on her wall so that when the employee entered her office she would be comfortable in the new environment. She also spoke to the employee in the Emotive channel, allowed the employee to paint her office a color of her choosing, and arranged for the employee to participate in a project outside the office one day each month. What were the results? The employee became a valuable team member, voluntarily took on mundane tasks that no one else wanted to do, and provided creative ideas to help the members of her team achieve their goals. One day shortly after the employee joined the branch, she confided to the authors that her new boss was the only person in the division who liked her. She added that when her boss was transferred, she intended to resign. Thus forewarned, we were able to ensure that each successor supervisor knew how to communicate with her and help her get her needs met positively. She continued to be effective and received several promotions and commendations.

Many of the inmates in juvenile detention facilities are Rebels. When they are confined to their rooms or when they are in lockdown, they agitate severely in some way, by banging on doors or walls, singing, talking, yelling, crying, or engaging in some other negative activity. Subconsciously, Rebels are experts at angering serious people such as Workaholics and Persisters. When in distress, they instinctively know which buttons to push and they push them regardless of consequences. Staff members in detention facilities usually respond to these outbursts by taking away privileges, but that does not stop the behaviors. In fact, in many instances, the negative behaviors increase. What might happen if instead of using punitive measures, staff members worked to deal with the inmates by helping them get their needs met in a positive way?

At the Ware Youth Center in Louisiana, staff members were trained in the concepts of Process Communication. In the six months after the training, there was a 44 percent reduction in student incidents compared to the corresponding six months the previous year and expulsions were reduced from 13 to two. There have been no expulsions in the three years since. Most importantly, they have a 25 percent recidivism rate, which is the best in the country. (The average for the United States is 68 percent and for juveniles who have committed serious crime, it is 80 percent.) Because of the success of their methods, the Ware Youth Center has been given responsibility for all of the juvenile detention centers in northeast Louisiana and recently built a facility to house the juvenile women in Louisiana who have been adjudicated to the juvenile justice system.

PROMOTERS

In first-degree distress, Promoters expect others to fend for themselves and do not support people who may need their support. "I'm going to make a man out of you if I have to break you in two trying." Or "Not tough enough, huh?" Or "If you can't stand the heat, get out of the kitchen." These are sayings that exemplify the spirit of first-degree Promoter distress.

An example of this is an Army colonel with a Reactor daughter who suffered from serious health problems and who was legally blind. Because he never supported her in anything, making her do everything for herself, the daughter felt that her father did not love her. She spent a lot of time in distress because she was not getting her Recognition of Person need met positively. After her father died, the daughter found a paper on which the father had written the names of all of his children with a brief comment about each. Beside his daughter's name he had written "Because of her blindness and poor health, I have to be hard on her so that she will be tough and be able to stand on her own two feet." He thought he was giving her the best gift he could give her, but all her life she felt that he did not love her and regretted having her as a daughter. Leaders must help their employees and their family members get their needs met positively if they are to be effective.

How do leaders invite Promoters out of first-degree distress? The Promoter's favorite channel is the Directive channel and their perception is Action. Leaders can say to them, "Tell me what you are going to do" or "Do this." Most of the time, Promoters will accept this invitation and will come out of first-degree distress.

What do Promoters do in second-degree distress? In second-degree distress Promoters put on a blamer mask and manipulate, con, make fools of others, set up fights or arguments between team members, tell lies about team members, engage in negative competition, and find ways to turn the tables on those they blame for things that have happened to them.

One of the authors, Joe, had a Promoter on his staff who had been advocating for a change in procedure to help the team accomplish one of its goals. He was right, but to accomplish this goal it was necessary to get several government agencies to assist the team. A meeting was scheduled in Joe's conference room. Joe started the meeting by explaining the need and describing what the team had been doing unsuccessfully to achieve the goal. He then introduced the Promoter to explain his plan. The Promoter looked at Joe, then at the group, looked back at Joe, and then back at the group. Finally he said, "We don't need their help. We can do it the way we have always done it."

What happened that resulted in the Promoter doing this? Three weeks before, Joe had asked the Promoter to prepare a briefing for the senior members of several government agencies. The meeting was held the previous Friday morning in Joe's conference room. The Promoter spoke for two hours and never once mentioned anything about the subject of the briefing. Finally, Joe interrupted him and ended the meeting. He apologized to the officials from the other agencies, took the Promoter aside so no one could hear him, and asked him why he did not speak about the subject he had been asked to brief on. The Promoter exploded angrily, and Joe called time, saying they were both too angry to discuss it at that time and suggesting they meet the following Monday. The next meeting took place before they could talk it out and the Promoter took the first opportunity he had to make Joe look bad.

This happened before the author had heard about the concepts of Process Communication. If he had understood the concepts of Process Communication, what could he have done? Because prevention is better than intervention, Joe could have used the Directive channel instead of the Requestive channel in giving him the assignment. Secondly, he could have given him explicit instructions about what he wanted the Promoter to cover. Third, he could have helped the Promoter get his need for Incidence met by explaining that this was a chance for him to look good and be known to senior officials of the various government agencies.

How could Joe have intervened after the fact? He could have apologized for getting angry and for not telling the Promoter exactly what he wanted him to brief on. He could have told the Promoter the officials had agreed to help, that being in charge of the new program would be a challenge, and that whoever ran the program would look good if it succeeded. He could have told the Promoter to tell him whether he was up to the challenge and wanted to lead the program. Joe did none of these things; the Promoter remained in distress for the next year and sabotaged everything he was doing in order to make Joe look bad, not realizing that he was only jeopardizing his own future. There is no clear thinking going on when people are in distress.

THIRD-DEGREE DISTRESS

What happens in third-degree distress? In third-degree distress all six personality types feel unloved, unwanted, and depressed. Workaholics reject others because they don't think clearly; Persisters cease to be team players and quit; Reactors stop caring about their appearance, their jobs, or their families; Dreamers shut down; Rebels find creative ways to get even; and Promoters abandon others. How can leaders invite people out of third-degree distress? Leaders can help them get their psychological needs met positively. Most of the time people will accept the invitation and will come out of distress. However, people who are in third-degree distress usually have been in distress for some time and will not have energy enough to stay out of distress for any length of time. To keep them out of distress probably will require enhanced interventions.

When leaders see the members of their management team or employees exhibiting any of these behaviors, they can be assured that the individual in distress will not understand what the leaders are saying to them. If the leaders are trying to implement a quality program, they must make every effort to invite their employees out of distress using these strategies in order for the employee to hear and understand the leaders' message.

As everyone knows, leaders also get into distress. What do leaders do in distress and what can they do to keep themselves from getting into distress? That is discussed in Chapter 10.

10

Leaders in Distress

"Effective leaders keep themselves out of distress by ensuring they get their psychological needs met every day."

Dr. Taibi Kahler

Leading an organization is stressful and leaders must get their needs met so that they stay in a positive place in order to think clearly and lead effectively. What do leaders of each of the six types do when they are in distress? We described several instances of leaders in distress in earlier chapters. In this chapter we will discuss what each type of leader does in distress and we will provide generalized action plans of things they can do to help them get their needs met both personally and professionally so that they can continue to be effective. Leaders who see themselves doing any of the things described in this chapter or in Chapter 9 can recognize that they are getting into distress and need to do something to get their needs met.

WORKAHOLICS

Workaholic leaders in distress attack people and over-control. They appear to delegate, but actually they micromanage. A division chief at an agency of the United States government was always in distress. He would tell his senior staff members what he wanted them to say in memos they were writing; as they were leaving his office, he would say, "I want to see it before it goes." When a staff member showed him a memorandum he would say, "That's not what I said" and then rewrite it. As a result, some staff members began taking their secretaries to his office with them and had them take down and type up what the division chief had said. Morale suffered and staff members began to say, "He's going to rewrite it anyway, so I won't spend any time on it." One day a staff member was about to leave for an important meeting at which he had a significant role to play. As he was leaving, the division chief summoned him to discuss a memorandum. The staff member knew that if he went to the division chief's office he would be late and might miss the meeting entirely. He went to the meeting and sent his secretary to the division chief's office. He was transferred the next day and had no regrets.

Workaholic leaders who see themselves doing these or any of the things listed in Chapter 9 can recognize these actions as warning signs of distress. They must do something to get their needs for Recognition for Work and Time Structure met positively. What are a few things Workaholic leaders can do to get their needs met positively? One leader used to keep on his desk a to-do list of actionable items. As he accomplished something, he crossed it off the list and said to himself, "Good job." He also planned his day, prioritized his tasks, and allowed plenty of time to get to appointments so that he never felt rushed or nervous about being late.

PERSISTERS

Persister leaders in distress point out to people what they are doing wrong and ignore what they are doing well. They attack people for their lack of commitment and attempt to push their beliefs on everyone. As a result, Persister leaders in distress can destroy the morale of an organization faster than any of the other types. Because of this arrogance and attacking manner, people don't do what Persister leaders want them to do, even when the Persister is right. Persisters who believe that no one shares their convictions and commitment ultimately may resign in disgust. A good example of this is the story in Chapter 8 about Myrla Cole Haury, the Board President of the Harvey County Domestic Violence/Sexual Assault Task force in Kansas.

Persisters in distress may also let their prejudices show as they attack others. For example, a division chief at an agency of the United States government was in severe distress. In staff meetings and meetings with division personnel he would belittle people and insult their heritage or culture. In short, he was an equal opportunity bigot. At one time 150 people worked for him, but because of his manner many of them transferred to other divisions. So many people transferred that the division did not have enough staff to properly do all of the work that was assigned to them. As a result, productivity decreased significantly and eventually he was transferred and forced to retire.

Persister leaders who find themselves doing these or any of the things listed in Chapter 9 must find a way to get their Recognition for Work and Conviction needs met positively in order to be an effective leader. What are some things they can do to accomplish this? Many Persister leaders become active members of civic or philanthropic organizations. Still others write letters to the editor on topics they are concerned about or write articles to pass on their values to the next generation.

REACTORS

Reactor leaders in distress have a hard time making decisions and often make mistakes. These mistakes may be silly, serious, and even tragic. In Chapter 6 we described the mistakes made by a Reactor CFO in a company in Virginia as a result of the dysfunctional management team constantly arguing and fighting during staff meetings. A Reactor leader in a government agency was faced with two deputies who had different views of a particular action they wanted the team to take. One of the deputies was responsible for the course of action and the other was not, but wanted to be. Neither would back down and the chief could not make a decision. As the deadline to implement an action plan approached, the chief called a meeting of the entire staff and had the two deputies explain their positions. The staff members wondered why they were there. "Just tell us what you want us to do," they said. That night the Persister who was responsible for the implementation drew up an action plan. He presented it to the chief the next morning and implemented it that afternoon.

These behaviors are warning signs that Reactor leaders are not getting their Recognition of Person and Sensory needs met positively. They must do something to get them met and get themselves out of distress in order to be effective. What are some things Reactor leaders can do to get their needs met? Many Reactor leaders eat lunch with friends at least weekly and set aside time each day in which they come first. They keep pictures of family in their offices and look at them often. They tell family members every day that they love them and ask for that message to be returned. Some people feel that asking for love negates the battery charge, but we disagree. The need must be met, even when it's necessary to ask for help.

DREAMERS

Dreamer leaders in distress shut down. They withdraw and become unavailable to staff members for advice and counsel. Walk-around management is not for them. For example, a Dreamer leader in a U.S. government agency was frequently in distress. She came to work in the morning, went into her office, and closed her door. She did not open it again until the end of the day unless she had to go to a meeting. She dealt with staff members who knocked on her door, but it was clear to everyone that she was uncomfortable dealing with people. Staff members stopped going to her and consequently she had no handle on what was happening on her team. Morale suffered and the team was not effective. Reactor members of the team felt she did not care about them. Workaholics were in distress because she did not ask them for information. The Persisters believed she was not dedicated and were distressed because she did not seek their opinions. The Rebels did not like her because she was aloof and no fun. The Promoters were in distress because she was so slow and deliberate that things did not move fast enough. The Dreamers were in distress because although she left them alone she never told them what to do. Productivity dropped off. Work that did get done was in spite of, and not because of, her leadership.

These behaviors are warning signs that Dreamers are not getting their need met for Solitude. Dreamers must find a positive way to get that need met if they are going to be effective leaders. What are some things Dreamer leaders can do to get their needs met?

One of the authors, Judy, gets her Solitude need met by gardening. The Dreamer phase principal of a large inner city private school gets her Solitude need met by coming to work before anyone else is there, enjoying at least 30 minutes to herself before she has to deal with the hectic activity of the day. At the end of the day, she goes for a long walk by herself. After her children go to bed, she reads books that interest her. Sometimes these are in her field and other times they are on subjects that fascinate her. Occasionally she writes poetry in her study. Another Dreamer, a Jesuit priest who is the head of a university department, has published several books of poetry. He also plays tennis and writes about it. These are just a few of the ways Dreamer leaders can get their Solitude need met.

REBELS

Rebel leaders in distress do not accept responsibility for their actions and blame everything that happens on others or on events beyond their control. They antagonize others and may deliberately or subconsciously sabotage the team or themselves. They may also resign from a position with an attitude of "I'll show you!" when they do not agree with decisions made by superiors.

A Rebel division chief in a government agency exercised each day by playing basketball. One day he fell and broke his arm while trying to get a rebound. He told everyone in the agency that the other division chief had deliberately broken his arm and continued to blame the division chief for nearly a year. He took it out on his family at home and was uncooperative with the division chief in the office. During staff meetings, he belittled the division chief by rolling his eyes, interrupting, and making sarcastic remarks. He opposed anything the other division chief suggested. Finally, the other division chief confronted him; they talked it out and then went out and had some fun together. The conflict was resolved and they became good friends.

In another instance, a Rebel project manager at a government agency was placed in charge of a large design project that had failed several times. Most of the members of the design team were Persisters, each of whom believed he was the only one who knew what design would actually work. Most of them had worked on the project for a number of years and during that time had developed a fair amount of personal and professional contempt for each other. The project manager read all of the research she could find and spent time talking with each individual. She listened closely to their proposed solutions and to their explanations of why the solutions offered by other engineers would not work. After listening to everyone and doing considerable research, the leader was convinced that the proposed system, as designed, would not work. She proposed an alternate design but was told by the members of the team that it would not work. They could not give reasons to support their opinions, but instead treated the leader with disdain because her design was different than anything they had considered.

The team leader met with the director of the center and told him that she believed they should explore other designs with other vendors to foster a spirit of competition and innovation. The director agreed, much to the displeasure of the members of the team. The leader asked another contractor to develop an alternate design. Meetings with the alternate design team were exciting, creative, and fun; in less than six months they were ready for a preliminary design review. The review went well and the leader was told that the alternate team's presentations were among the best the agency had ever seen. Even so, for political reasons they would go with the other design. The leader was directed to assemble key players of the design team and develop a plan to make the design viable.

The leader was in severe distress at the decision. She called the entire team together and the traditional team presented their plan for discussion. The leader listened and then said that she had no confidence in their design and that she would not support their plan. She resigned as program manager and team leader. Her attitude at the time was "Ill show you. I'll quit." Did the plan succeed? No. It failed.

Rebel leaders who see themselves doing these or any of the behaviors described in Chapter 9 must recognize that they are not getting their need for Playful Contact met positively and that they must do something professionally or personally to get the need met. What can Rebel leaders do to get their need for Playful Contact met? When Joe was in a Rebel phase he always walked to another person's office rather than call first to ensure the person was in. As he walked through the halls, he got his Contact need met by speaking to everyone he passed, whether he knew them or not. He had fun posters on his walls. Once in the middle of a seminar, a client told him they were only going to pay for half of the people attending. Joe became very angry and, to put it mildly, was not at his best with everyone that afternoon. Realizing he had not met his need for Playful Contact for a couple of weeks, that night he went to a pub and enjoyed a battle of two bands playing loud, fun music. The next day he explained to everyone what had happened, apologized for not being his usual self, and invited them to learn a lesson from his negative example. Everyone must get their motivational needs met in order to be effective.

PROMOTERS

Promoter leaders in distress manipulate, con, and make fools of people. Frequently, they set team members competing with each other rather than encouraging cooperation among all sectors of the organization. This was the management style of a Promoter who was chief of a large office in a U.S. government agency. He criticized senior staff members in staff meetings and encouraged negative competition. He acted as if he were above the rules of common decency. For example, he sent one mid-level member of his staff on a two-week trip and entered into an affair with the officer's wife while he was gone. The result was that some members of the staff lost respect for him, others became yes-men to curry favor, and one, a Promoter, told lies about the staff members he considered to be the main competition for his next promotion. When people became aware of the lies and denied them, the office chief did not force the Promoter to retract the lies. The office staff became completely dysfunctional and little was accomplished.

In another instance "Jack," the Promoter CEO of a high-tech subsidiary of a U.S. company, was invited to meet with the President of the United States at the White House. The president of the parent company was also invited. The President invited Jack into the Oval Office for a private meeting, leaving the president of the parent company, also a Promoter, outside on the lawn. He was livid and got even by firing the senior members of the subsidiary staff. When Jack later called an early morning news conference to announce a major technological breakthrough, he invited the president of the parent company to attend with him. The president accepted. The night before the press conference, Jack wrote a letter of resignation and went on a trip, leaving the president of the parent company, who had no knowledge of the breakthrough, to deal with the press.

When Promoter leaders see themselves engaging in these behaviors, they must be aware that these are indicators of unmet needs. What can Promoter leaders do, either personally or professionally, to ensure they get their need for Incidence met in a positive way? A Promoter CEO founded a company in Canada. That was exciting and he was getting his need for Incidence met while growing the company. As the company grew and became more profitable, he lost interest and sought a change of direction. He sold the company for a very nice profit and founded another company. When that company became successful, he did the same thing. This time his change of direction took him to Europe to drive racecars on the Grand Prix circuit. After a few years, he changed direction again and returned to the United States to found another company.

To be effective, leaders must not allow themselves to get into distress. They can avoid distress by ensuring they get their needs met every day. When one person in distress is confronted by another, situations deteriorate.

Another way of saying this is, "A mask invites a masked response." Leaders cannot allow themselves to accept the invitation into distress because nothing good will come of it. As we saw in Chapter 9, people in distress are not capable of thinking clearly; effective leaders must be able to think clearly at all times.

Leaders also must be able to communicate to be effective. Consider Dr. Kahler's rule of communication: "When there is an offer and an acceptance in the same channel, communication will take place." When either party is in distress, that party wears a mask and is not in a channel. There is also a rule of miscommunication: "When either the offer or the acceptance is not in a channel, miscommunication will take place." This means not only that leaders must not allow themselves to get into distress. They also must ensure that those with whom they want to communicate are not in distress. The implication is clear. When people are in distress, effective leaders must invite them out of distress in order to achieve effective communication. The strategies for doing this are explained in Chapter 9.

AN EXAMPLE

At a mid-sized public electronics supply company in the Midwest, there was conflict between the Board of Directors and the management team. The Board members were Persisters, Workaholics, and Promoters; some were in a Promoter phase. The board members were major shareholders and were more involved in the day-to-day management of the company than are many boards. There was conflict and miscommunication between the various members of the board and they were resistant to change. Because they were not keeping up with technological advances, the company was losing market share and profitability.

The board hired a new CEO who believed that the concepts of Process Communication are strong tools for developing emotional understanding and robustness among those who use the concepts in positive ways. The CEO also believed that managing the board would be critical in order to turn the company around. The CEO did four things:

1. He put the entire management team through Process Communication training.

2. He had the team carefully think out how they would present all proposals to the board for approval.

3. He hired a consultant company to train all levels of the company in the concepts of Process Communication.

4. The CEO told the management team that if anyone got into distress during a meeting, someone would call timeout. They would take time to get everyone out of distress before going on with the discussion. In the first month, they averaged about four timeouts per meeting. By the second month they were only calling timeout about once per meeting. By the third month, there were no timeouts called and the team functioned very smoothly. Within 18 months they improved profitability and had about $5 million in cash reserves. They also cleaned out about $1.5 million of inventory.

In an effort to persuade the board to use a new methodology to manufacture their products, the team carefully thought out their approach. Because many of the board members were in distress, the CEO and the team knew the board members' initial reaction would be to refuse to approve any proposal for change. The team knew they had to anticipate the objections of the various board members and provide information about how the new technology would benefit the company in ways that were acceptable to each board member. At the same time, they had to assure the board members that it would be possible to continue to use the old technology that the board favored.

When they presented the proposal to the Board, the CEO explained that the new technology would cut costs, thereby improving the profitability of the company. He also explained in general terms that the company would still be able to use the old technology "around the edges." The CEO was able to answer all of the objections and questions satisfactorily and the Board approved the proposal. Within 18 months the company improved their market share from 30 percent to 70 percent.

If the CEO and the team had allowed themselves to get sucked into distress in response to the distress of the board members, they would not have succeeded. From time to time, the CEO himself was in distress. By understanding this, he was able to get his needs met and get himself out of distress. This made a huge difference in his ability to respond to the board and to his staff members more effectively. It also enabled him to ensure that all members of the team stayed out of distress too. In this way, they were able to develop strategies to help the various board members get their needs met. They were able to deal with each board member in that person's favorite perception and provide the information each member needed in ways that were acceptable to them. In doing so, they were able to improve the profitability of the company.

This is how effective leaders communicate. They help people get their motivational needs met every day and they individualize the way they communicate, using each person's favorite channel and perception.

Happy processing.

Index

Page numbers in *italics* refer to tables or illustrations.

T-U-V

W-X-Y-Z

Belong to the Quality Community!

Established in 1946, ASQ is a global community of quality experts in all fields and industries. ASQ is dedicated to the promotion and advancement of quality tools, principles, and practices in the workplace and in the community.

The Society also serves as an advocate for quality. Its members have informed and advised the U.S. Congress, government agencies, state legislatures, and other groups and individuals worldwide on quality-related topics.

Vision

By making quality a global priority, an organizational imperative, and a personal ethic, ASQ becomes the community of choice for everyone who seeks quality technology, concepts, or tools to improve themselves and their world.

ASQ is...

- More than 90,000 individuals and 700 companies in more than 100 countries

- The world's largest organization dedicated to promoting quality

- A community of professionals striving to bring quality to their work and their lives

- The administrator of the Malcolm Baldrige National Quality Award

- A supporter of quality in all sectors including manufacturing, service, healthcare, government, and education

- YOU

Visit www.asq.org for more information.

ASQ Membership

Research shows that people who join associations experience increased job satisfaction, earn more, and are generally happier.* ASQ membership can help you achieve this while providing the tools you need to be successful in your industry and to distinguish yourself from your competition. So why wouldn't you want to be a part of ASQ?

Networking

Have the opportunity to meet, communicate, and collaborate with your peers within the quality community through conferences and local ASQ section meetings, ASQ forums or divisions, ASQ Communities of Quality discussion boards, and more.

Professional Development

Access a wide variety of professional development tools such as books, training, and certifications at a discounted price. Also, ASQ certifications and the ASQ Career Center help enhance your quality knowledge and take your career to the next level.

Solutions

Find answers to all your quality problems, big and small, with ASQ's Knowledge Center, mentoring program, various e-newsletters, *Quality Progress* magazine, and industry-specific products.

Access to Information

Learn classic and current quality principles and theories in ASQ's Quality Information Center (QIC), *ASQ Weekly* e-newsletter, and product offerings.

Advocacy Programs

ASQ helps create a better community, government, and world through initiatives that include social responsibility, Washington advocacy, and Community Good Works.

Visit www.asq.org/membership for more information on ASQ membership.

*2008, The William E. Smith Institute for Association Research

ASQ Certification

ASQ certification is formal recognition by ASQ that an individual has demonstrated a proficiency within, and comprehension of, a specified body of knowledge at a point in time. Nearly 150,000 certifications have been issued. ASQ has members in more than 100 countries, in all industries, and in all cultures. ASQ certification is internationally accepted and recognized.

Benefits to the Individual

- New skills gained and proficiency upgraded
- Investment in your career
- Mark of technical excellence
- Assurance that you are current with emerging technologies
- Discriminator in the marketplace
- Certified professionals earn more than their uncertified counterparts
- Certification is endorsed by more than 125 companies

Benefits to the Organization

- Investment in the company's future
- Certified individuals can perfect and share new techniques in the workplace
- Certified staff are knowledgeable and able to assure product and service quality

Quality is a global concept. It spans borders, cultures, and languages. No matter what country your customers live in or what language they speak, they demand quality products and services. You and your organization also benefit from quality tools and practices. Acquire the knowledge to position yourself and your organization ahead of your competition.

Certifications Include

- Biomedical Auditor – CBA
- Calibration Technician – CCT
- HACCP Auditor – CHA
- Pharmaceutical GMP Professional – CPGP
- Quality Inspector – CQI
- Quality Auditor – CQA
- Quality Engineer – CQE
- Quality Improvement Associate – CQIA
- Quality Technician – CQT
- Quality Process Analyst – CQPA
- Reliability Engineer – CRE
- Six Sigma Black Belt – CSSBB
- Six Sigma Green Belt – CSSGB
- Software Quality Engineer – CSQE
- Manager of Quality/Organizational Excellence – CMQ/OE

Visit www.asq.org/certification to apply today!

ASQ Training

Classroom-based Training

ASQ offers training in a traditional classroom setting on a variety of topics. Our instructors are quality experts and lead courses that range from one day to four weeks, in several different cities. Classroom-based training is designed to improve quality and your organization's bottom line. Benefit from quality experts; from comprehensive, cutting-edge information; and from peers eager to share their experiences.

Web-based Training

Virtual Courses

ASQ's virtual courses provide the same expert instructors, course materials, interaction with other students, and ability to earn CEUs and RUs as our classroom-based training, without the hassle and expenses of travel. Learn in the comfort of your own home or workplace. All you need is a computer with Internet access and a telephone.

Self-paced Online Programs

These online programs allow you to work at your own pace while obtaining the quality knowledge you need. Access them whenever it is convenient for you, accommodating your schedule.

Some Training Topics Include

- Auditing
- Basic Quality
- Engineering
- Education
- Healthcare
- Government
- Food Safety
- ISO
- Leadership
- Lean
- Quality Management
- Reliability
- Six Sigma
- Social Responsibility

Visit www.asq.org/training for more information.